ENGLISH

GCSE Grade Booster

Stephen Papworth

Schofield & Sims Ltd.

0 7217 4610 1

First printed 1989
Reprinted 1998

Schofield & Sims Ltd.
Dogley Mill
Fenay Bridge
Huddersfield
HD8 0NQ
England

Typeset by Ocean, Leeds
Printed in England by Antony Rowe Ltd, Chippenham

Contents

Acknowledgements

The author and the publishers wish to thank the following for permission to use copyright material:

Barnaby's Picture Library: p.32

Introduction

How To Use This Book

This GCSE Grade Booster is a new type of revision book for GCSE English. You should keep the book by you from the beginning of your course to the end, so that you can consult it whenever you tackle a new type of work, especially one which is giving you problems. It is not a complete English course, but it concentrates on the types of writing, comprehension and oral tasks that you often find in GCSE assessments, along with some of the language problems that go with them.

Read through the book quickly from cover to cover in order to find out what it contains, and where. As you read, some sections will already stand out as ones which will be of help to you: make a note of them for further study, and return to them later.

Keep this Grade Booster handy for the rest of your English course, and each time you start a new assignment or task, look up the relevant advice in the book: it should be like having *two* teachers for the subject – one in the classroom, and one you can carry around with you! You will also find this book an invaluable help to refresh your memory when you embark on your final revision.

It is not possible to include *every* sort of skill or exercise required by every syllabus in a book of this length: I have concentrated on the key skills demanded by the National Criteria for GCSE and the most common ways of assessing them. It is up to you (and your teacher) to discover what your particular syllabus demands, and to use this book to help whenever it can. Often, I have taken care to explain to you *why* a particular type of exercise is set, as I believe it helps to know the reason behind what you are doing, especially if it seems odd, eccentric or 'arty' to you. English teachers may well be an odd bunch, but generally there is a good reason behind what they are asking you to do.

Many readers of this book will be taking a GCSE English syllabus which does not involve sitting any exams at all, whilst others will be doing a mixture of coursework and exams. Each way of doing your GCSE has its advantages: coursework-only syllabuses keep your nose to the grindstone all the time, whereas ones with an exam component may make you pull out all the stops on exam day – or, alternatively, reduce you to a nervous wreck! If exams do make you nervous, try the relaxation exercises mentioned in Chapter 7.

Taking English Examinations

Preparing for an English exam consists mainly of working conscientiously through the course you have been given. Shortly before the exam, reading through this book two or three times, together with any notes you have made, will help to keep your knowledge of techniques fresh in your head. Otherwise, pay attention to your favourite vices – the habitual mistakes that consistently attract red ink on your work.

In particular, practise

- punctuation exercises
- problem spellings
- problem types of comprehension questions.

Make sure that you know what to expect on each examination paper you are sitting.

At a more practical level, check that you have two good pens for the exam (one may break or run out), a pencil for writing notes and plans, and a watch for timing. You may or may not be allowed to use white correcting fluid for your answers; in any case, it is quicker simply to cross things out, and if your work is basically neat, crossing out will not lose you any marks.

Check through the general format of the paper to see that it is *exactly* what you have expected. How many questions are there? How many questions must you answer in each section? Then read *all* the instructions carefully, and, as you come to them, each question. Is the question you have chosen as easy as it seems? Probably it is, but you should take care to check that you really understand it. And then, enjoy writing your answers as much as you can. Let your imagination loose, and get absorbed in your task – though keeping one eye on the clock. Finally, if you have time, check your work: it is surprising how many mistakes creep in when you are working quickly.

I hope this book will help to boost your grade in all your assessments and examinations, whatever form they take. Work at them seriously, but also try to get as much enjoyment as possible out of them, as this will motivate you to try harder and work better. Enjoyment generally helps you to produce good results in English, and much of this comes from letting your imagination out into your essays and orals. Good luck with your studies, and enjoy them!

1 Ways with Words

Words

To many people, the ability to communicate in words – to talk, to write, to think – is what sets human beings apart from the rest of creation. Words are extremely important and extremely flexible tools for understanding things, allowing us to express facts and feelings, and even to say things which are purely imaginary. Because of this, the first parts of this chapter are about how to develop a wider vocabulary and how to pick up all the aspects of a word's meanings.

Since words are subtle, the mistakes we make with them are subtle, too. This chapter goes on to examine some of the mistakes people make, and to explain how to avoid them.

Vocabulary

The Words You Have to Choose From

Your vocabulary is the total number of words you know. Obviously, the more words you have to choose from when you speak or write, the better chance you have of saying what you want clearly.

Developing a Wide Vocabulary

The most important aid for this is to have the right attitude: to be interested in new and unusual words. If you are not interested, you simply will not learn many new words. If words do capture your imagination, you will enjoy learning them, knowing that you will soon use them and be able to say new things. You can try to learn words as you find out their meanings, but it is really helpful to keep a notebook so you can go over them when it suits you best.

- Treat each new word as a new opportunity for expressing yourself.

Dictionaries

Choosing One to Fit Your Needs

Dictionaries come in all shapes and sizes: how do you choose the best one for you? A pocket-sized dictionary will be easy to carry around with you, but you should also have a larger one to keep by your desk. Go to a bookshop with a wide choice of dictionaries on display, and look up in each of them a word you have just learnt. Is the definition easy to understand? Is it set out clearly? Is there so much detail that you cannot find the part of the definition that you want? Or does the definition miss out some things that you already know about the word?

- Buy the dictionary with the longest entries that you really understand!
- Every dictionary has lists of the abbreviations and signs used in it, and the marks which are used to indicate pronunciation. Find these and learn them.

Meanings

Words Have More Than One Meaning

When you look up almost any word in a dictionary, you will see that it usually has more than one meaning listed after it. How do you choose the right meaning? Naturally, you try to fit the meanings in the dictionary one by one into the passage in which you found the word. Only the meaning which makes sense in the original word's surroundings (or *context*) can be the right one. You can use this fact to help you to guess meanings when you do not have a dictionary with you. Your guesses will be only rough ones, but since you made them up yourself, you will remember them. The next time you see the word, you will be able to test your guess and make it more accurate. This is a very important way of picking up new vocabulary: let's see how to do it.

> *When my brother came into the room, he didn't say anything, but I knew by* intuition *what was wrong: he had quarrelled with Anna. I could see it in his whole behaviour, for nothing else would have made him so downcast.*

The context to the puzzling word, *intuition*, is full of clues: we can see that it involves being able to guess at things without being told them, and we can ourselves guess that this is its meaning. We are not too far wrong, either: one dictionary gives the following definition:

> intuition *n* 1. a feeling that one knows without understanding how or why 2. immediate insight.

There are some more examples of this kind of guesswork in Chapter 4.

- Guess meanings intelligently, using clues from the context, such as similarities to other words, and partial explanations.
- Refine your guesses every time you meet the new word.

The Feelings Behind Words

Synonyms

Often, a whole list of words may seem to have the same meaning, and it may be difficult to know why one has been chosen, and not another.

For instance, all the words in this cartoon could refer to the very same animal. Words like these, which have broadly the same meaning, are called *synonyms*. Such words do not have exactly the same meanings as each other, however: there are differences in the feelings and attitudes they carry with them.

Meanings and Feelings

We can divide the meanings of a word into two parts:

1. its basic meaning, which you might expect to find in a dictionary:
   dog: four-legged animal which barks
   bow-wow: four-legged animal which barks
   canine: four-legged animal which barks;
2. the feelings and attitudes which are associated with it:
   dog: This is a fairly neutral word which does not convey much by way of feeling.
   bow-wow: This conveys the idea that the animal is friendly and lovable; it is the view of the dog that we might use to reassure a child.
   canine: This represents the view of the dog species that a scientist might have: it is cool and technical.

It is extremely important to be able to tell how *formal* or *informal* a word feels. An informal word is one which you would normally only expect to find in speech between people who know each other closely: thus *bow-wow* is an informal, childish term, as is *pussy-cat* or *bunny-rabbit*. Formal words are ones which you can use in front of strangers, and be sure that the words will not seem odd, childish or embarrassing – for example, *dog* or *canine*. You might like to work out which of the words in the following lists are informal and which are formal.

mum	copper	fag	telly
mummy	bobby	cig	TV
mother	policeman	cigarette	television

If you choose a word with the wrong feeling, you can look silly:

> *"I must charge you," said the constable, "with having an uncontrolled and vicious bow-wow."*

It is a good idea, then, to try to guess at the types of feeling a new word can put over. Again, you do this by checking with the context. Here are some points to watch for:

- Is the word being used to express approval or disapproval?
- Is the word polite or rude? childish or adult? formal or informal?
- Is the word slang, dialect, or ordinary English?

Poor Vocabulary

Slang

> *"When I speak to my friends and family I use slang all the time. Everybody understands it, so why can't I use it in writing?"*

English teachers very often hear this objection when they ask pupils not to use slang in their essays. There are several points to be made about it.

1. *Slang is not always understood.* Some forms of slang are used only by one age group or one social group: *you* may know that the police are called *the fuzz*, but do your parents, or your grandparents?
2. *Slang brings an informal mood with it.* Slang is the vocabulary of everyday conversation, of intimacy, of personal feelings, and as such it is often out of place in written work, which is more formal.
3. *Slang can be used in direct speech* to make it more realistic – but it works well only if there is a contrast between the slang in your dialogue and the formal language in the rest of the story. A character may *say* "I've got a new bike", but when writing you would normally refer to it as a *bicycle*.

Colloquialisms

These are expressions which are not quite slang, but which still have an informal feel to them and which we usually expect to find in speech rather than in writing. Again, they should be avoided outside direct speech, unless you are trying to create an informal, friendly mood.

Some examples are:

The short forms of verbs: *I'm* for I am, *she's* for she is, and so on; padding phrases such as *isn't it?*, *well*, or *if you see what I mean*; words used with a meaning different from their basic one, such as *fantastic, terrific,* or *tremendous*.

Dialect

Dialect words are ones used in a particular district. Words such as *owt* and *nowt* (anything and nothing) used in Northern England, or Cockney rhyming slang such as *titfer* (tit for tat, hat), are examples. Again, they bring an air of informality with them, but have the disadvantage of being completely meaningless to some English speakers. They need using with great care, even in direct speech.

- Tabloid newspapers constantly use slang, colloquial language and dialect to make them lively. Do not copy their style in everyday written work.
- Slang, colloquialisms and dialect are basically spoken forms of language. Use them for special effect only.

Weak Words and Clichés

Some of the words we use in colloquial language are so vague as to be almost meaningless. When we say something is *nice*, we are saying very little other than we like it. The word has become weak through over-use, as have many terms of approval or disapproval – for example:

all right
awful
fabulous
fantastic
great
terrific
tremendous

Other phrases referring to quantity or quality are also weak and over-used:

quite
lots of
loads of
miles of
ages and ages

The verb *to get* is very weak and can usually be either left out or changed. The informal ''John's got a bike'' can be written out as ''John has a bicycle''; ''Get it cleaned up'' becomes ''Clean it up''; and so on.

Clichés are set phrases which recur constantly. Many of them are comparisons:

as tired as a dog
as big as an elephant
as sharp as a knife

- These phrases have become worn out by over-use, so avoid them.
- If you have written a comparison like the ones above, try changing its second half – for instance, *as sharp as broken glass*.

Some clichés take the form of pairings of words, where both halves of the phrase seem always to come together, for instance:

a lovely day
a breath-taking view
a delicious meal
a kind thought.

- If you have written phrases like these, try changing the first word of the pair into another word, or developing it into a phrase. For instance:

  a sunny, breezy day
  a view over the whole county
  a meal that stimulated our tastebuds
  a charitable thought.

Problem Words

There are some words and phrases which time and time again cause an outbreak of red ink on examination papers, usually owing to differences between formal and colloquial usage. Here are the most troublesome.

All right — This phrase is colloquial and vague, and should be avoided in formal writing. Note the spelling: *alright* is wrong.

Different from/ Different to — Do not write, for example, "Her sweater is *different to* mine." Use *from*, not *to*, with *different*, as in "Her sweater is *different from* mine."

Kind of — Besides being colloquial in tone, this phrase shows up vague thinking: if you saw something which was "kind of exciting", can you not express what it was like more precisely? The same applies to *sort of*.

Lay/Lie — These words are endlessly confused. In the present tense, if a person stretches out flat, he or she *lies* down (not *lays*); if he or she places one thing on something else (for example, a cloth on a table), he or she *lays* it down. On the other hand, the *past tense* of "he or she lies down" is "he or she *lay* down", whilst the past tense of "he or she lays it down" is "he or she *laid* it down". The following table will help you:

	present tense	past tense
stretching out (e.g. on a bed)	lie	lay
putting down (e.g. on a table)	lay	laid

Me — *Me* is often crossed out by teachers in two circumstances:
1. After *it is*. "It is me" is colloquial; use "It is I" in formal speech and writing (also, "It is he", "It is she").
2. In phrases such as *me and my friend*. It is considered rude to put yourself first, and forms such as "my friend and me" are preferred. Secondly, you need to check whether "me" or "I" should be used in the sentence. This is easily done by ignoring the reference to the friend or other person; for example:
My friend and me were going home
Pretend the friend wasn't there: you get
Me was going home.
This is rubbish; you would really write,
I was going home.
Therefore, your full sentence must be
My friend and I were going home.
Try this check on the following sentence:
Don gave the letters to my girl-friend and me.
You should be able to see that this sentence is correct, and does not need changing.

Off of — Sentences such as "I jumped off of the log" are not acceptable in formal English. You can do without the *of*:
I jumped off the log.

OK/Okay — Colloquial and vague. Try to express *why* you liked or approved of the thing you are describing. Notice that *OK* is the correct form.

Sat/sitting — "I was *sat* on a park bench" would normally be corrected to "I was *sitting*". Why? Because *to be sat* means that someone else put you in position, whilst *to be sitting* means simply that you happened to be there.

The table below may help. Compare this entry with the one on *stood/standing*.

to be put in position	*to remain in position*
to be sat	to be sitting

should of — this is incorrect, as is *would of*. Always write *should have* and *would have*. If you make this mistake, it is because you are hearing the colloquial forms *would've* and *should've* in your head as you write.

Stood/ Standing — The difference between these words is similar to that between sat and sitting. "She was *standing* in the corridor" would mean that she just happened to be there, and was not walking around. "She was *stood* in the corridor" would mean that someone had stood her there. This table may help.

to be put in position	*to remain in position*
to be stood somewhere	to be standing somewhere

What — Your work will be corrected if you write sentences like these:
It was a book what my aunt gave me.
My camera is better than what yours is.

Both these forms are very colloquial, and are looked down on by educated speakers.

1. Never use *what* to link parts of a sentence other than questions; always use *which* or *that* instead:
It was a book which my aunt gave me.
2. Never use *what* after *than*; simply leave it out.
My camera is better than yours is.
3. The main use of *what* is to *start questions*:
What time is it?
What are you doing?

Would of — As in the case of *should of*, this error is caused by mishearing. It is the result of trying to write down "would've", which is a contraction of *would have*. Always write it as "would have", in full.

Numbers and Abbreviations

Another usage problem comes with the inclusion of numbers and abbreviations in your work. It may seem strange to find figures crossed out, when everyone can read them, and it may be really annoying to find yourself criticised for using abbreviations which you have just painfully learnt in another lesson! The reasoning behind the correction of both these features is similar, however, and is connected once more with creating the right tone.

Numbers

The use of numerals is thought to be more appropriate in business, scientific and technical writing than in personal or imaginative pieces. Thus, we can accept the use of figures in Example 1 below, but not in Example 2.

1. *You will need a 6-volt battery.*
2. *It was a lovely Easter: I was given 7 eggs.*

Example 2 should be written with the word 'seven' instead of the figure 7, because it is a personal, not a scientific or technical, statement.

On the other hand, statements involving numbers which need more than two words tend to be written with figures even if the context is personal or imaginative, so that both the following examples would be right.

1. They had over a hundred Christmas cards.
2. There were 121 different kinds of sausage in the shop window.

Abbreviations

These are thought to be appropriate *only* in business, scientific and technical writing; avoid them totally in personal and imaginative work. There are three exceptions to this rule:

1. Cases where the *full written form* for the abbreviation has fallen out of use – for example, *Mr* and *Mrs* – or cases where there is no fully spelled equivalent, for example, *Ms.*
2. Abbreviations which can be *pronounced and written as words* (these are known as *acronyms*):

   He worked at Unesco.
3. Abbreviations which are so familiarly used that their full forms are seldom written and it is not necessary to insert full stops in them:

   BBC, ITV, GCSE.

- Figures and abbreviations belong in business, scientific and technical work.
- Imaginative and personal writing uses full words whenever possible.

Spelling

Rules or Chaos?

English spelling does have rules, believe it or not! After all, we all know one of them:

I before E except after C (when the sound is EE).

The problem when writing about the rules is that most of them are so complicated that you get lost in trying to put them on paper: it is even worse trying to learn the rules in this way.

In fact, almost everyone learns all the spelling rules unconsciously, without trying: the human mind seems to be built that way. The words which cause teenagers and adults trouble are the ones that do not follow the rules, or do not follow them in the most obvious way. Fortunately, there is only a limited number of such words in common use, and it is possible to learn a list of them by heart, if you try. Some lists are printed below: I would suggest that you test yourself on twenty words a week, and try to learn the ones you get wrong. Do not look at the list first: ask someone to read the words out to you.

The Hit List

Here is a list of words which all cause GCSE students a great deal of trouble.

accelerate
accommodate
acquire
aerial
assassin
awkward
bachelor
bicycle
business
catarrh
cellar
cemetery
character
college
committee
definite
develop
diarrhoea
disappear
dissatisfied
embarrass
exaggerate
exceed
exhilarating
February
foreign
government
handkerchief
hypocrisy
independence
irrelevant
jewellery
khaki
laboratory
leisure
lieutenant
manoeuvre
Mediterranean
miniature
minutes
necessary
neighbour
pastime
pigeon
possess
precede
preferred
privilege
probably
proceed
professional
pursue
receive
recommend
restaurant
rhythm
seize
separate
sergeant
silhouette
sincerely
skilful
succeed
surprise
tragedy
twelfth
unnecessary
veterinary
weird
wilful
woollen
yacht

Confusions

When there are two or more words which sound alike, we spell them differently. The problem, of course, is remembering which is which! Ask a friend to test you on the following sets of words. He or she can tell you the pronunciation and the clues printed after them; you will have to get the spellings in the right order.

1a. *allowed* (permitted)
b. *aloud* (loudly)
2a. *bare* (naked)
b. *bear* (wild animal)
3a. *boar* (wild pig)
b. *boor* (ruffian)
c. *bore* (uninteresting person)
4a. *break* (shatter)
b. *brake* (slow something down)
5a. *coarse* (not fine)
b. *course* (what a race is run on)
6a. *cue* (stick used in billiards)
b. *queue* (line of waiting people)
7a. *gorilla* (big ape)
b. *guerrilla* (terrorist)
8a. *hear* (perceive through your ears)
b. *here* (not there)
9a. *its* (of it)
b. *it's* (it is)
10a. *knew* (past tense of knowing)
b. *new* (not old)
11a. *lightening* (getting lighter)
b. *lightning* (comes with thunder)
12a. *muscle* (strong body tissue)
b. *mussel* (shellfish)
13a. *naval* (to do with the navy)
b. *navel* (tummy-button)

14 a.	*passed*	(what you do to exams)
b.	*past*	(As in, "She drove past the house")
15 a.	*peace*	(goes with quiet)
b.	*piece*	(a part)
16 a.	*principal*	(most important)
b.	*principle*	(basic law or belief)
17 a.	*quite*	(wholly)
b.	*quiet*	(goes well with peace)
18 a.	*rain*	(wetness)
b.	*reign*	(what the Queen does)
c.	*rein*	(on a horse)
19 a.	*right*	(correct)
b.	*write*	(put on paper)
20a.	*their*	(belongs to them)
b.	*there*	(not here)
c.	*they're*	(they are)
21 a.	*waist*	(round your middle)
b.	*waste*	(left overs)
22a.	*weather*	(rain, sun, etc.)
b.	*wether*	(castrated ram)
c.	*whether*	(or not)

23a.	*which*	(goes with who, whom, whose and that)
b.	*witch*	(magical woman)
24a.	*your*	(belonging to you)
b.	*you're*	(you are)

- Once you've learnt these . . . don't confuse them!

2 The Secrets of Sentences

Sentences

A sentence is a series of words which, when spoken or written, can stand alone and make complete sense. We all have been taught this definition and, in fact, most of us talk and write in acceptable sentences. The problems usually start when we try to recognise what a sentence is as we come to punctuate it. In addition, the fact that you *can* write sentences does not necessarily mean that you always write the most effective ones. Both of these problems can be helped by studying the types of sentence which exist and the ways in which they can be fitted together.

Types of Sentence

Simple Sentences

It is easy to recognise short sentences when they stand alone, and equally easy to punctuate them. If a sentence expresses one idea, and has just one verb in it, we call it a simple sentence.

The cat sat on the mat.
Jack and Jill went up the hill.
A stitch in time saves nine.
Is he coming?

Each of these makes sense on its own and is therefore awarded the usual capital letter and end punctuation (full stop, question mark or exclamation mark).

Minor Sentences

Often, when we speak, we say a single word rather than a complete sentence: this is usually in reply to someone else's question, command or statement.

"Are you ready?"
"Sure."
"Go to bed."
"No!"

These words make complete sense when taken with the sentence they are replying to, and are called minor sentences. They are given the usual capital letter and end punctuation.

Is it correct to use minor sentences in written work? Sometimes. (I have just used one.) If you are writing out some conversation, minor sentences will help to make it more natural; in other types of writing, they may be used occasionally to create special emphasis.

Compound Sentences

The most basic way of writing longer sentences is to join simple sentences together with the conjunctions (joining words) *and* and *but*. These two words act as links, and the two or more parts of the sentence joined by them are of equal importance.

The cat sat on the mat and the dog lay on the rug.

Jack and Jill went up the hill but there was no water.

I went into town and looked in the supermarket but there was no unsalted butter.

We often string sentences together like this when we talk, but in writing the effect can be monotonous because we do not have the sound of a speaking voice to vary the way the words are emphasised.

Other useful links include *either . . . or*, *neither . . . nor*, and *not only . . . but also.*

Complex Sentences

It is possible to join ideas together into sentences so that one idea becomes the main idea in the sentence and the others become subordinated to it. The complex sentence is the key to a fluent style, and increases the expressiveness of your writing, so mastering it is of the greatest importance. In addition, use of complex sentences will help you avoid the most common punctuation error, as we shall see later.

In order to write complex sentences, you need to use a number of conjunctions, which come in two groups:

1. *Who, whom, which, that.* If you have two sentences which are about the same person or thing, you can often join them with one of these words.

   John came into the room. He looked ill.
   →*John, who came into the room, looked ill.*
   or
   →*John, who looked ill, came into the room.*

   Agnes smiled at me. I shall always be grateful to her.
   →*Agnes, to whom I shall always be grateful, smiled at me.*

   The boat passed Castle Duart on its way to the Isle of Skye. It was an unforgettable sight.
   →*The boat passed Castle Duart, which was an unforgettable sight, on its way to the Isle of Skye.*

   This is the dog. It bit your little girl.
   →*This is the dog that bit your little girl.*

Notice how in the first and third examples the new sentences are *more precise* than the old ones. In general, complex sentences show the relationships between ideas much more clearly than other types.

2. *When, whenever, until, till, since, after, before, while, whilst, where, wherever, for, because, as, therefore, so, so that, in order that.*

   This is a fairly large class of words and phrases, many of which you are bound to use already. Make sure you are familiar with them.

   Using these conjunctions often involves moving parts of the sentence around, and altering the occasional word. This is, in part, what prevents development of the sense of monotony which exists in long strings of compound sentences.

   Hopkins went into the room. He would stay there for the next twenty-four hours.
   → *Hopkins went into the room, where he would stay for the next twenty-four hours.*

   You must wait until six. I shall come back then.
   → *You must wait until six, when I shall come back.*

   We shall need a pound of gelignite. If we don't have it, we shall never get into the safe.
   → *We shall need a pound of gelignite, because if we don't have it, we shall never get into the safe.*

- Develop your use of subordinating conjunctions. Keep the list in front of you as you write.

A Faulty Type of Sentence

There is one way of writing sentences which is not acceptable in formal English. This is probably the greatest single cause of corrections on students' work, and it usually shows itself as a correction of punctuation, like this:

Full Stops!

The night was cold and dark. John shivered as he walked down the alley(,) he was both frozen and frightened. He remembered the report of the attacker(,) he could not get the picture of his evil face out of his mind. He came to the last corner(,) it was a blind one and he could not see round it. He passed it quickly(,) at last he was in the light(,) soon he would be home.

Here we seem to have five sentences, four of which have one or two commas in them. Why have they been corrected? Look at the four sentences, and you will see that each of them could be written out as two separate ones:

The night was cold and dark. John shivered as he walked down the alley. He was both frozen and frightened. He remembered the report of the attacker. He could not get the picture of his evil face out of his mind. He came to the last corner. It was a blind one and he could not see round it. He passed it quickly. At last he was in the light. Soon he would be home.

It is because of this that the commas have been corrected, as it is a firm rule of punctuation that *commas cannot separate possible sentences.* Normally, sentences must be separated by full stops or joined by the conjunctions mentioned in the previous section.

Why is this mistake so common? Probably because we often speak like this in hurried, informal speech. We may *say* a series of short sentences with only short pauses between them, but we should never *write* them.

You may feel that the 'correct' version shown above reads jerkily or bittily because of the stronger punctuation. This is where the use of compound and complex sentences is important, since they allow you to join ideas together in different ways and give your passage a feeling of fluency. Compare the second version of the passage with this final one:

The night was cold and dark. John shivered as he walked down the alley, for he was both frozen and frightened. He remembered the report of the attacker, and could not get the picture of his evil face out of his mind. He came to the last corner, which was blind, so that he could not see round it. He passed it quickly. At last he was in the light, and soon he would be home.

- Never separate sentences by using commas.
- Use a variety of sentence types in your writing.

The Sounds of the Comma and the Full Stop

Commas can be used to separate parts of sentences, and represent a particular sort of pause. Many pupils are told that a comma represents a short pause, and a full stop a long one, but the facts are a little more complex than this. Listen to an expert reader – a newsreader, for instance – and try to identify two sorts of pause:

1. the *short pause*, the spoken equivalent to the comma. The voice often stays quite tense or high-pitched;
2. the *long pause*, which represents the end of a sentence. The voice often drops on the last syllable or two before the reader stops: this is because he or she is relaxing, coming to the end of a sentence. Here we have the spoken equivalent of the full stop or question mark.

Now listen to the voices of your friends and family: you should be able to recognise the two types of pause in everyday conversation. All fluent English speakers use them naturally, without thinking. Finally, read out a short passage and make a cassette recording of it. If you can recognise these two types of pause in your own reading voice, and in the inner voice which thinks as you write, you will soon master the use of the comma and the full stop.

- Listen to your inner voice as you write: do your sentences sound varied and correct?

Punctuating Speech

The rules for the punctuation of speech are quite rigid, and examination candidates frequently make mistakes with them. Fortunately, they are easily learnt if you set your mind to it.

Inverted Commas (Speech Marks/Quotation Marks)

Everyone knows that when you write out the exact words which someone is saying, you have to put them in inverted commas. The only basic problem is whether to use single inverted commas, like this:

'Oh what a beautiful morning!'

or double ones, like this:

"Oh what a beautiful day!"

You will see either form of punctuation in books, and the choice is up to you. Once you have made your choice, however, stick to it. Do not mix both the methods in a single essay.

The problems come when you add a phrase such as "he said", "she shouted", or "they called" to attribute the speech to someone. Now, look at two basic examples.

1. *Anne said, "Let's go to the disco."*
2. *"Let's go to the disco," Anne said.*

In 1, we have simply taken Anne's words and the punctuation that goes with them, and put them in inverted commas:

"Let's go to the disco."

Then we have put *Anne said* in front, punctuating the pause between the two with a comma:

Anne said, "Let's go to the disco."

Number 2 isn't quite so easy, however, as the full stop after *disco* has turned into a comma. Why? Try reading the sentence with a full stop after *disco*: it sounds too disjointed, too jerky, and besides, it doesn't make sense.

Question marks and exclamation marks are not turned into commas:

2a. *"Shall we go to the disco?" Anne asked.*
b. *"Go to the disco!" Anne shouted.*

There are two other ways in which speech can be punctuated:

3. *"If you're going to the disco," John said, "we might as well all go."*
4. *"Anne's going to the disco," John said. "We might as well all go, then."*

Search for the differences in these versions. Number 3 has a comma after *said*, and a small w for *we*, whilst Number 4 has a full stop after *said* and a capital W for *We*. Pause for a moment to try to work out why this is.

In Number 3, a single sentence was spoken:

"If you're going to the disco, we might as well all go."

Accordingly, the punctuation is light, to allow the quoted sentence to read all as one.

In Number 4, two separate sentences were spoken:

"Anne's going to the disco. We might as well all go, then."

The full stop and the capital letter are used to keep the sentences separate.

- Try to memorise the four different patterns of speech punctuation by sight, and recall them as you write.

  Speech punctuation: the four patterns

  1. Anne said, "Let's go to the disco."
  2. "Let's go to the disco," Anne said.
  3. "If you're going to the disco," John said, "we might as well all go."
  4. "Anne's going to the disco," John said. "We might as well all go, then."

Layout of Speech

When you write out conversations there is one further tricky thing to remember: every time anyone starts to speak, you start a new paragraph, no matter how short this makes your paragraph look.

> *"What do you call a six-foot wrestler who steps on your foot?" Darren asked, as a smile of anticipation crossed his lips.*
>
> *"I don't know," Michelle replied, looking him quizzically in the face.*
>
> *"Sir!" said Wendy.*
>
> *"Oh no, you've heard it!" laughed Darren.*

Note that the paragraphs are indented properly.

- Each speech forms a paragraph on its own.

3 Creative Writing

Essays

Sometimes pupils ask why they have to write essays: you do not find essays in the real world, outside the class-room, they say. Actually, this is wrong: essays surround us everywhere.

An essay is, quite simply, a piece of writing with a single subject. It can be as short as a paragraph or as long as a book. Almost everything you read is an essay in this sense: newspaper stories, magazine articles, short stories, chapters from books – all of these are written in the same way as a class-room essay, so the basic skills of essay-writing are essential to everyone who writes.

Paragraphs

Essays are divided into paragraphs, each of which deals with a single aspect of the main subject: we can call these aspects topics. A paragraph can be as short as a single word

No!

or as long as you want it. The paragraphs in popular newspapers tend to be very short. Mostly, though, paragraphs will be 80-120 words long, and they nearly always have more than one sentence.

If you write lots of short paragraphs, your work will be bitty and jerky to read; if you write long ones, your reader will not have enough opportunities to rest, and may get bored or confused.

If you are having trouble in writing paragraphs which are long enough, you need to develop your topics. Many paragraphs start with a sentence which announces the paragraph's topic (this one does). This is called the *topic sentence*. After this, you need more sentences to help make sense of the topic.

- Go for
  - descriptive detail;
  - narrative detail;
  - supporting evidence;
  - conclusions drawn from the topic;

  depending on the type of paragraph you are writing.

Essay Plans

Every essay needs to be thought out carefully, and most people benefit from writing plans on paper. The very least you need is a list of likely topics for paragraphs.

MOST PEOPLE BENEFIT FROM HAVING A PLAN.

Let us suppose you were set the topic *A Journey I Shall Always Remember:* you could start by jotting down ideas on a piece of paper. It is best to put them down in *random order*, or you will be tempted to put them into your essays in the order in which you thought them up, which may not be the best. Leave plenty of white space around them, for new ideas.

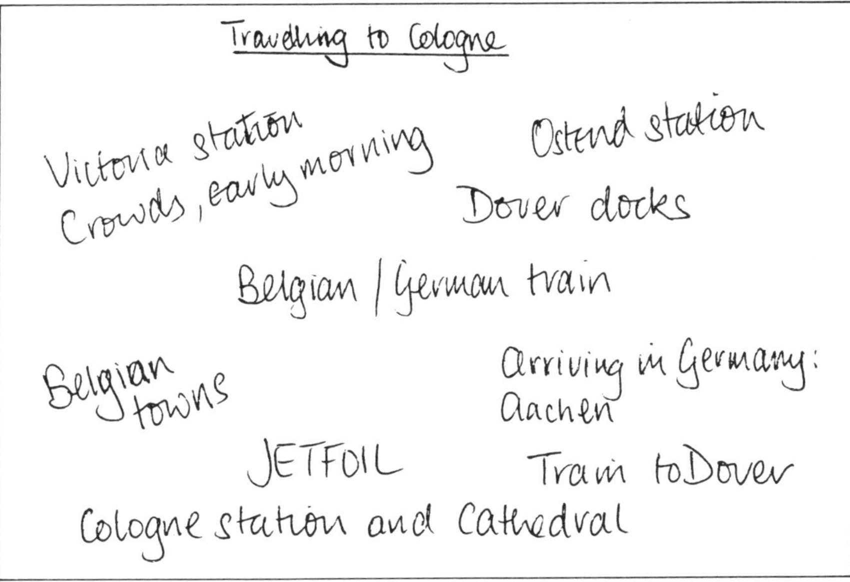

Travelling to Cologne

Victoria station
Crowds, early morning

Ostend station

Dover docks

Belgian / German train

Belgian towns

arriving in Germany:
Aachen

JETFOIL

Train to Dover

Cologne station and Cathedral

The next step will be to work out how you could develop each idea. Jotting down brief notes under each heading will help, or you may like to do this in your head – especially if you are working quickly in an exam. You may decide at this stage that you have too many ideas, or too few, so you can cross some out, or add some. Then you can sort out an order for the paragraphs and number them.

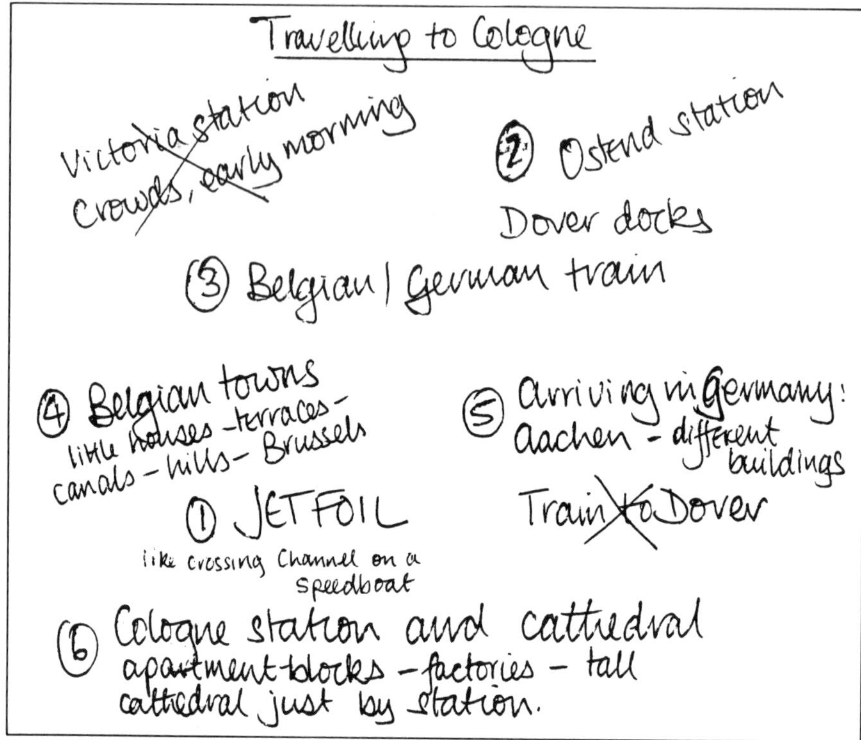

For another example of a plan worked out like this, see *Argument Essays* (page 46). This is, of course, not the only way of arriving at a plan from a set of random ideas. If you already have a method which works for you, continue to use it or try this in addition. The important thing is to develop a method which enables you to change the order of your ideas as you go, until you have found the plan which works best.

Three-Part Plan

One vital question to ask is whether your essay begins and ends effectively. Teachers often say you should plan three sections:

Introduction;
Development;
Conclusion.

This is another way of saying that your essay should:

- begin interestingly in a way which lets the reader clearly know the subject *or* arouses his or her curiosity;
- have a middle section which follows on naturally from the ideas in the introduction, and which has some form of organisation within itself;
- end interestingly, in a way which makes the reader feel your treatment of the subject is complete.

You may find that your introduction and conclusion already figure in your plan, or you may wish to add new paragraphs to top and tail your essay.

- Begin and end your essay on strong, interesting points.
- Check that all your ideas come in a natural, organised sequence.

Lists of Essay Titles

Sometimes, especially in examinations, you will find yourself faced with a mixed list of essay titles, like this:

1. "It was my happiest hour." Write about an event or a situation which you might describe in this way.
2. Write a short story containing the following lines:
"A cold sweat broke out on her forehead as she heard the sound. At first she felt paralysed, but slowly she forced herself to turn round."
3. Should smoking be banned in all public places?
4. The Open Air.

The first thing is to work out what types of essay each title will permit. Some titles are highly specific, such as number 3. Here, only an argument essay will do. Numbers 1 and 2 appear to invite a personal experience and a fiction story respectively – but is this really true?

Could you build number 1 round someone else's experience? Or could you even make it up from scratch? Remember, what is wanted is a good essay, and not necessarily the literal truth. In number 2, although a short story is asked for, it could equally be built round a true experience. Question 4 is the widest of all – a truly open question, which invites you to write in any way you choose.

- Ask yourself: How open is each question? What are its widest possibilities?

Writing from Pictures

This is another exercise in opening up possibilities. Always study the question or instructions which come with your picture: they may be highly specific, or they may simply invite you to write in any way which the picture suggests to you. For instance:

1. Look at the photograph and write an essay of any kind which is inspired by it;

or

2. Write a story in which the scene shown in the photograph occurs.

Pictures can be of great help in finding inspiration for something to write about. Photographs, in particular, contain a wealth of information. Scan the picture you have been given carefully, and look for the following features:

- *Characters.* If there are any people in the picture, what are they like? What can you tell from their
  - facial expression?
  - posture, way of walking, and so on?
  - clothes and possessions?
- *Backgrounds.* Pick out as much detail as you can about the place shown in your photograph.
- *Situations.* People together in one place are generally relating to one another: talking, looking at one another, sharing an activity – even pointedly ignoring one another. Imagine your way into the situation.
- *Time and Season.* You can often tell a great deal from tiny details of a picture, such as the way the light is falling, the way people are dressed, whether trees are bare or covered in leaves.

Take time to explore your picture before picking up your pen.

Description

The cottage was one of a row of four, built out of large blocks of pink sandstone, which sheltered beneath a small plantation of wind-bent Scots pine trees. In front was a tiny garden with a place to park our car, and a pocket-handkerchief patch of unkempt lawn with enough room for a couple of deckchairs. Its hedges were a riot of rambling roses already in bloom. The front door opened with a creak, and led us straight into the living-room, which was simply furnished but clean and tidy; its centre-piece was a black iron range, which had an aromatic pine-log fire laid in it, ready to light if the evening turned cool. We breathed sighs of contentment: the room was everything we'd been hoping for.

Types of Description

You may be asked to write a descriptive essay – about a place, say, or a person, or even a building, as above; on the other hand, description plays a part in almost all narrative (story-based) writing, too, to bring it alive.

- Always ask yourself *why* you are describing something. Is it
  - to make the reader see, hear or smell the subject in his or her mind?
  - to convey a mood or feeling?
  - both of the above?

If you are describing something for a scientific or technical purpose, you will concentrate purely on the senses, but if you are writing to entertain or involve your reader, you also need to concentrate on your feelings.

The Five Senses

We are aware of things through our senses:

sight;
hearing;
smell;
taste;
touch.

In all description, we should try to make the reader imagine our subject through the senses.

- Before you write, imagine your subject as vividly as you can. Picture it in your mind; try to hear it, smell it, touch it, in your imagination.
- List nouns, adjectives and verbs which appeal to your senses as you plan your work.

Think about

sight: shapes, colours, light and shade, textures;
sounds: loud and soft, musical or harsh, peaceful or alarming;
smell: rank or sweet, pleasant or unpleasant;
taste: sweet or sour, strong or delicate, delicious or revolting;
touch: softness and hardness, roughness and smoothness, heat and coldness.

Now look for colour, sound, smell and touch in the description on page 33.

Detail

Whatever words you use, the most important factors in any description are the details. Vague statements such as *It was pretty* or *We liked the cottage* put over an attitude, but do not describe. In the description of the cottage, you are asked to imagine details such as the roughness of the lawn, the roses, the door creaking, and the smell of the logs. Observed details such as these bring the description to life.

- Use plenty of observed detail.

Mood

> *The next morning we were woken early by a brightness coming through the thin curtains. We jumped out of bed and ran to the window: the sky was already pure blue, with only one or two tiny puffs of cloud. The meadow across the road was emerald green,*

and the barley-field beyond a pale gold. The birds were singing loudly in the hedges, and even the surface of the road was winking and glittering at us. We turned to each other and smiled.

Often, the point of a description is not merely to make something appear in the reader's imagination, but also to make him or her feel something about it. The passage above, for instance, tries to re-create a moment of happiness.

To do this sort of description well, you need to imagine in particular the feeling that you are trying to put over: try to capture it as strongly as you can while you write. Think your way into the scene you are describing, and try to get your body to respond to the feelings you are

imagining. Become an actor in the scene – and then let your mind choose the right words and details for you. Before you put pen to paper, think out – or even make lists of – comparisons and synonyms which will help express your feelings.

- Imagine feelings as you describe things; get as involved as possible. BUT, if you do this, check your spelling and punctuation later on, as you may not have been paying much attention to them!

Character Descriptions

How can you give detail about someone's character? It is easy to describe a person's looks, but what about his or her nature?

My grandmother was the queen of her kitchen: I can still remember her sitting at the centre table swathed in a huge old-

fashioned white apron, with her sleeves rolled up and a rolling-pin in her hand, smiling and surrounded by the products of a baking day. There would be jam tarts the size of saucers, pies, sponge-cakes, gingerbread men, and – best of all – moist, treacly Yorkshire parkin. Slowly she would survey the day's work, and smile gently with weariness and contentment: she had fulfilled her duty as the family's purveyor.

Body Language

We all communicate our personality and our current mood through body language, which ranges from obvious things such as facial

POSTURE AND CLOTHING ARE VIVID SIGNS OF A PERSON'S CHARACTER

expressions and gestures, through our choice of clothing, to more subtle aspects such as posture, ways of walking and moving, and the way we use our eyes. Think how downcast eyes make us believe a person is shy, whilst a direct gaze can be almost threatening. In describing a character, try to go for habitual gestures, postures and expressions, and observe what is characteristic about your subject's style of dressing.

In the passage, I have tried in part to put over my grandmother's character by describing her clothes, her expression and her posture, as she surveys her day's work.

- Describing body language is an immediate way of letting your reader see inside a character.

Background Information

More information about my grandmother comes from the description of the things surrounding her: the large kitchen table, and the size and quality of the things she had baked. Their surroundings often tell us a great deal about people, especially if they have created those surroundings, or if the surroundings have influenced them. People's homes and gardens, their places of work, private rooms, the pubs and clubs they go to, their schools and colleges, can all throw light on their inner beings.

- Set characters against a background of their everyday life, or of their special achievements. Link them with the places to which they belong.

The Power of the Story

One of the most valuable ways of characterising someone is to tell *anecdotes* (very short stories) about them. These work well even in the middle of a description, so long as you do not let any one story run away with you and dominate an essay. A well-chosen anecdote can, on the other hand, provide a good climax to an essay on a character.

> *My grandfather, on the other hand, was king in his shop, which sold bicycles and electrical goods. I'll always remember one of the assistants coming to him for help when he was having tea in the back room. "Fuse wire?" he roared. "Do you think I'm going to disturb my cup of tea for a twopenny thing like that? Send the customer away!"*

- Use anecdotes to tell us what someone's actions are like.

The Spoken Word

What does your subject's voice sound like? What sort of language does he or she use? What does he or she habitually talk about? Try to capture these exactly on the page, so that your reader can really hear your character's words. Imitate the length of their sentences, for instance, and, within limits, whether they use slang or dialect. (This is one of the few occasions when it is acceptable to use these forms of language in writing. Nevertheless, take care not to write anything offensive!)

> *"You'd better get your dinner now," my Grandma would say to me if Grandfather was late. Sooner or later we would hear him come in the back door.*
>
> *"Hello, Mother," he'd shout, "we were busy wi' customers."*
>
> *"Aye, well," she'd say, looking him straight in the eye. "Your dinner's in the dog!"*

Dialogue like this is not truly description, but it does add colour and mood to a character essay.

- Use speech to tell your reader not only *what* someone always talks about, but *how* they sound, too.

Stories

Telling stories is probably one of the favourite pastimes of the human race. We tell them to our children, read them, listen to them on the radio, and watch them every night on television. The cinema industry is based on them. Not all stories, of course, are imaginary. Newspapers and news broadcasts consist largely of true stories, and history is one continuous narrative. Perhaps the most popular category of story is the one embracing tales we tell about ourselves and people we know, when we gossip.

What is the fascination of the story? Probably story-telling is our most basic way of making sense of life. Though we do not always make it obvious, every story has a meaning, and tells us something about the story-teller's view of life. On top of this, stories let us live, imaginatively, other people's experiences – they start our imaginations working, which is a pleasure in itself.

English teachers set you stories partly because they are usually fun to write, if you relax and let your imagination out, and partly because they hope that your imagination will develop through reading and writing. But there is more to it than that: because stories involve human feelings, they give you an excellent chance to explore the expression of feelings in language, which is an important skill. Finally, since almost all stories will contain patches of description, narrative and dialogue, they allow you to try your skill at a wide range of types of writing.

- Have fun imagining your stories.
- Think about why you find them interesting.
- Pay attention to the feelings you are expressing.

Personal Experiences

We all gossip – about ourselves, and about each other: it is one of our ways of understanding human behaviour. Writing true stories can work in a similar way: when we write them down, we have to think about what we want to say and decide what the story is really about, so that eventually we understand it better. Maybe it will help the reader understand people better, too, as well as amusing him or her.

Topics like the following give you a chance to tell about your experiences:

1. Write about an occasion when you were the centre of attention.
2. "*Least said, soonest mended*." Tell the story of a time when this saying came true in your life.
3. Write a chapter from your autobiography.

The first thing to do when faced with a title such as one of these is to

think of an incident, of course – something that sticks in your memory as comic, dramatic or significant. Then the hard work starts.

- Ask yourself
  - why you like the story and why your reader might like it;
  - whether there was a lesson or some other meaning you might draw from the story;
  - what emotions the story contains.

When you have answered these questions, you will know what to stress when you write.

- Ask yourself
  - how you can make the meaning plain to the reader;
  - how you can express the characters' feelings.

Here is a miniature personal experience story.

Lost in London

I must have been about five when I first realised that adults weren't perfect, and they didn't know everything. My mother and I were on holiday in London together – not for the first time, as we had relations down there – and we were walking down some deep canyon of a street lined with tall, black buildings and laden with pedestrians and traffic. That year it occurred to me how big London must be, and that I'd no idea where we were. Suddenly I broke out in a cold sweat! We were lost, I was sure of it. I'd no idea at all of how to get back to Grandma's flat.

"Mum," I said tremulously, "do you know where we are?"

"Of course I do!" came a confident-sounding reply.

"Do you know how to get back to Grandma's?"

"Oh, we just have to find a tube station, and get on a train!"

That was it! Find a tube station! She didn't really know where the next one was. I was sweating again. And would the trains go to the right places?

"Where is the nearest station?" I asked in a whisper.

"Just down at the end of this street," she said.

I walked on, with bated breath. After a minute or two, she pointed to a stairway. "There it is!"

I was limp with relief: I trusted my mother again – but for the first time, the seeds of doubt had been sown.

Meanings

One of the simplest ways to put over a story's meaning is to show your characters coming to a recognition, or learning a lesson, through what they do, or through what happens. You can do this by letting them talk about it, or by telling the reader what they thought. In the story you have just read, the realisation is mentioned twice, at the beginning and end.

Characters

Stories depend for their effect on our being able to imagine the characters in them clearly. When you are writing about yourself, this is not usually a problem, as your character will generally emerge from the reactions you describe. The characters of other people may well need sketching in, though. In *Lost in London* I have only hinted at my mother's confidence and competence, but this is enough. You may need to describe a character briefly, but the best characterisation comes from people's actions, words, thoughts and reactions (see *Character Descriptions,* pages 35 – 36).

Background

The setting of a story can be very important. A sense of background will make any story seem realistic, and in other cases the setting is essential to the story: the whole point of the experience on page 00 is that it took place at a certain age in a certain place. In GCSE work you will not have a great deal of space to spend on description, so:

- Ask yourself what is essential about the story's setting, and how you can put it over briefly.

In the London story, I confined the background information to saying how we came to be there, and one sentence about the size and bustle of the street.

Feelings

Feelings can come out of the story in many ways. Sometimes the

descriptive words you choose will do the trick; at other times, you might like to mention what the characters felt. Often, describing someone's bodily reactions – blushing when embarrassed, for example – can be very powerful. Also, the dialogue that your characters speak is often the key to their feelings.

For all of these techniques, the important thing is that you imagine the feelings as strongly as you can when you write: that way, your mind will usually choose the right words for you.

Shaping Your Story

Many stories stick to a plan like the basic three-part plan of any other essay (page 31).

- *Beginning* (exposition). Here you have put over your basic background, and perhaps some characterisation, before setting the action in motion. In the example on page 39, this all takes place in the first paragraph.
- *Development.* Now you tell the story, scene by scene. In longer essays, you need to pace the material carefully, deciding what the important points are: these you can describe in full, complete with dialogue. The rest can be summarised more quickly.
- *Crisis and Resolution.* The crisis is the climax of the story, where the important action takes place. Usually it comes near the end. The resolution rounds off the story, telling us what happens after

the crisis. Often the resolution also contains the characters' realisations and recognitions.

- Stories should be planned: it helps to prevent them from becoming boring and over-long.

Fiction

Everything already said about personal experiences applies equally to stories which you have made up. There are, however, a couple of extra points which are important.

Characterisation

In an imaginary essay, it is unlikely that you yourself will be the hero or heroine, so you will need to pay extra attention to characterising him or her. This does not necessarily mean writing a description of the character, though you may want to do this. (If you do so, keep it short, so as not to slow the story down.)

> *It was Friday evening, and Henry Austin looked round the crowded railway carriage with interest and satisfaction. Almost every seat was taken by people like himself, heading towards their homes and families for the weekend. He thought of his wife, Lisa, and their twin three-year-old daughters, Kate and Gemma; he felt a smile cross his face. There would be time to relax, time to play with the children. That was what he needed: a long, restful weekend.*

The characterisation in this passage comes from our seeing what is going on from the character's *point of view*: we look round the carriage as Henry Austin would, we listen in on his thoughts, experience his feelings. An alternative way to do this would have been to have written as if the writer were Henry Austin:

> *It was Friday evening as I looked around the crowded railway carriage. I enjoyed watching the other people, who were, like me, heading home for the weekend . . .*

Writing like this can produce really vivid results, but it means that you can write only from one person's viewpoint: you cannot add any comments of your own.

You should think a lot about your main character – who he (or she) is, what he does, where he lives, what his family are like, how he dresses. You will not need to put all of this in the story, but knowing it will make you understand him or her better and write more vividly.

- Keep character descriptions short.
- Consider whose viewpoint you are using.
- Get to know your hero or heroine fully.

Plot

Plots revolve around *problems*. Will the boy be right for the girl? Will the astronauts survive an encounter with the aliens? These problems provide us with the *suspense* which keeps us reading or watching; and in the course of the story, the problems are resolved, either happily or tragically. Of course, during the story it should not be obvious what the ending will be, and things will happen which act as red herrings for the reader and the characters. A typical short plot might run:

We meet the characters and get to know the problem;
they do something to solve the problem, but things get worse;
they carry on;
things reach a crisis;
there is a happy ending.

You can sharpen up your writing by thinking in these terms. Note that problems can come either from inside a character – from his or her feelings – or from the outside world.

Before you write:

- Define the problem at the heart of your plot.
- Think of the possible misfortunes as well as successes which your characters may have.
- Link your ideas about plot to the realisation or meaning behind the story.

Argument Essays

Putting over Points of View

Often you will come across questions which ask you to give your views on a topic or to discuss a controversial statement.

1. *"The young people of today have no respect for their elders."* What are your views on this subject?
2. *"Unless more care is taken of the environment, our descendants will be living on a desert planet."* Discuss this viewpoint.

Questions like these ask you to argue knowledgeably over viewpoints, and so it is important that you have *facts* on which to base your arguments. It is also useful to know what arguments other people have used about the subject. You can get this knowledge in four ways.

- In coursework or classwork, your teacher may go over the subject with you. Pay attention! Make notes!
- You may be given printed information to use. Read it thoroughly, and underline or note down the ideas which seem most important.
- Research the topic in your school, college or local library. This takes time, but can be very worthwhile.
- Talk the topic over with your classmates, parents and friends – but do try to work out who is being sensible and who is not!

Making a Point

It is a good plan to think of each paragraph of your essay as making a single point, and work out how you are going to make that argument convincing. Normally, the best technique is to start by announcing the point that you are going to make!

> *Sometimes people from the older generation can be really annoying; they do not realise that life is different these days from when they were young.*

- Then you need to develop your point, to make your reader believe it. You can do this in one or more of the following ways.
- Explain what you mean: go over the ground again in more detail, or in simpler language.
- Give scientific proof: use established facts and figures to prove your point.

> *A survey in the* Sunday News *last month said that 63% of all teenagers felt that their parents did not understand their difficulties.*

- State facts from your experience: support your idea with personal knowledge which may illustrate your point even if it does not prove it!

> *I have heard of several young people whose parents call them lazy or feckless because they haven't been able to get jobs, when the truth is that they have tried repeatedly to find work.*

- Compare or contrast your idea with something similar and well known.

Probably the same thing happened to our grandparents when they could not find work in the depression of the 1930s. It was different for our parents in the 1950s and 1960s, though, when there was full employment.

- Appeal to authority: give the views of someone who is well known, or who has inside knowledge of the field you are writing about.

  Mr. Dennis Lyons, a social worker who talked to the class, said that he thought it is always hard for older people to see things from the viewpoint of the young, and that young people always have problems like this whenever society is changing.

Of course, you will not always use *all* of these methods: usually one or two is enough!

Planning Your Essay

More than in any other sort of essay, the order of ideas is important in an essay of argument. The ideas must relate to one another, or your essay will read like a series of random jottings on the subject.

Beginning an Argument Essay

Once again, the safest way to begin is to make it clear just what your essay is about. In the first sentence or two, it is a good idea to do one or more of the following:

- Explain what you think the question or essay-title means.
- State the basis of the two sides of the controversy you are discussing.
- State the case you are arguing for.

Otherwise, your introduction should probably tell the reader of the importance of the subject you are tackling. It may be important to you personally, or to the world at large.

Developing Your Argument

The middle of your essay will vary according to whether you are trying to:

put one side of the argument,

state both sides of an argument in a balanced way

or

put one side but also counter possible objections from the other.

The first case is the easiest, so we shall start with that. On a piece of paper, jot down the basic ideas you have. Put them down in any order, all over the paper, not in a neat list. This will make is easier for you to experiment with the order in which you want the points to appear in your essay.

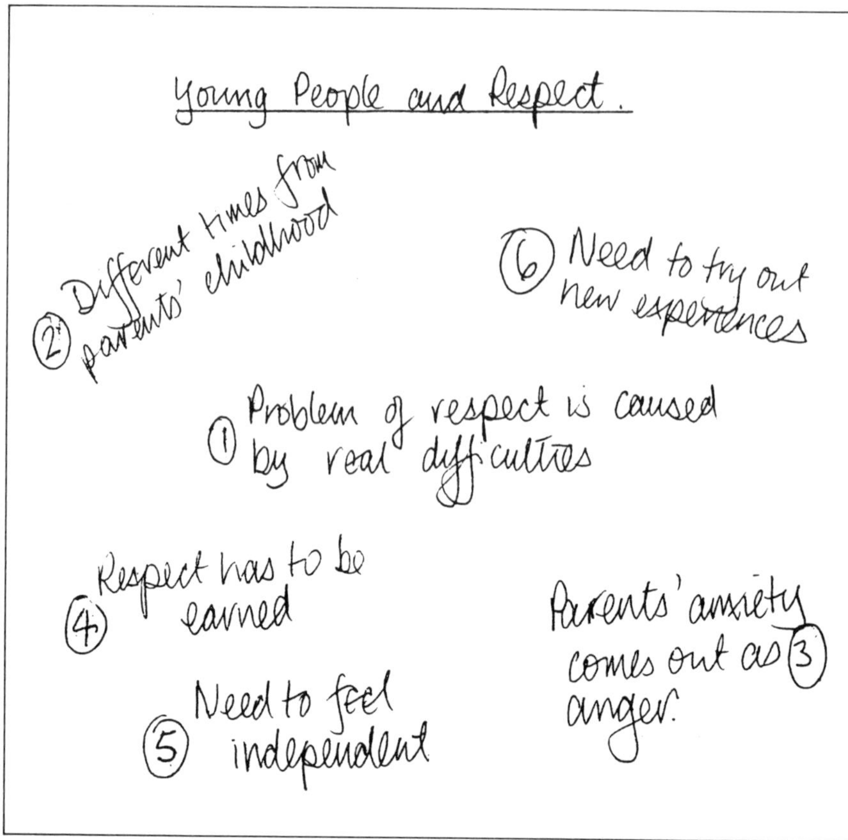

When you have written down five to eight headings, think about them carefully. Consider how you could develop each idea. Which can you make most interesting? Do any of these ideas belong together, because they are similar? If so, can you write a paragraph on each, or can you join two ideas into a single paragraph? Choose one of your most striking points and number it 1, so that you can use it in the first paragraph of your development. Make the connected ideas come straight after it, then go on to your other ideas, numbering them one by one. It helps if you can save a good one until last. In the sample plan, I have grouped points about parents first (1-3) and young people second (4-5).

In essays where you state both sides of a case, you can try to balance each paragraph by putting in a point and its opposite, or you can write the middle of the essay in two sections, first putting one case and then the other. The second option is much the easier! The same is true if your essay is basically one-sided, but you wish to answer objections which other people might make to some of your points.

Signposting

Remember to show how your points relate to one another, especially if you are doing a two-sided piece. The following words and phrases help:

in addition
moreover
in support of this
nevertheless
on the other hand
on the contrary
despite/in spite of this
for example
to illustrate this

- Use a plan.
- Think about the order of ideas and the links between them.

Concluding

Your last paragraph should, of course, state some conclusions – even if they are that you cannot decide which side you are on! Sum up the reasons for your final position in order to support it.

- The end of an argument essay should clearly show the reader what your views are.

4 Practical Writing

Writing with a Purpose

The tasks considered in this chapter all consist of writing which is meant to communicate something specific – usually factual – to its reader, rather than to express the quality of your imagination. They deal with writing with an aim or a purpose, and one of the main skills involved is to make that purpose clear in your mind. Sometimes, they deal with writing for a specific reader, or type of reader; who these are, and what they are like, also needs considering.

A final quality which these tasks have in common is that each has its own format or plan, which has become accepted over the years. You need to learn these formats to perform the tasks correctly.

Perhaps the best single piece of advice about this type of exercise is to take it seriously: make believe that you are doing the task in the real world. For example, if you are asked to write a letter to an aged aunt, imagine as realistically as possible that you are doing so; or if you are writing an article as if for the local paper, make sure that you study an actual copy of the newspaper before you set pen to paper. Success in these exercises depends to a large degree on how realistic your answers are.

Letters

Types of Letter

There are three basic types of letter, and though they have some similarities, it is essential to be able to know the differences between them:

1. *Personal letters* – the ones you write for social reasons to your family and friends;
2. *Business letters* – letters written to or by businesses and organisations to get things done;
3. *Letters for publication* – letters to the editors of newspapers, to agony columns, and so on.

Personal Letters

There is a great deal of variety within this kind of letter: think of the difference in tone between the following types:

1. *Dear Snuggly,*
   Ooh, I'm missing you. We had a wonderful day out on Saturday, didn't we? Too bad you live so far away . . .
2. *Dear Mrs Green,*
   I want to thank you and all Class Five for the lovely present. It is standing on my hospital cabinet as I write now, looking at me with its pink eyes . . .
3. *Dear Aunt Lynn,*
   Thank you for your lovely letter. It's really good to know that Jill has settled into her new college, and is making friends . . .

Type 1 consists of informal personal letters between people who know each other very well. In these, anything goes – jokes, hints, private codes, slang: it is up to you and the person to whom you are writing to decide what you like. You will naturally not be asked to write letters like this for your GCSE!

Type 2 consists of formal social letters sent to older people and acquaintances. In these, your spelling and correctness count, as they are ways in which the reader forms an impression of you. You have to judge the *tone* well, to achieve the right level of politeness, and you have to judge what you write about, so that it will be interesting to your reader.

Type 3 is the sort of formal personal letter you are most likely to be asked for in GCSE – one in which you describe what has been going on in your life to a friend or relative who does not see you from day to day.

Planning

In real life, personal letters often tend to be bitty – a paragraph about this, a paragraph about that – though sometimes they will develop one main subject which takes over the letter. For assessment, you are usually asked to write about one central experience, as in questions like this:

> *Imagine that you are on a long holiday abroad. Write a letter to a friend at home, describing what you have been doing.*

You might do best to limit the number of events you tell about, and focus mainly on one major topic: this will give you the chance to write more expressively.

Correctness

In reality, you might write in the intimate style of a Type 1 letter, depending on who you are writing to. For assessment, imagine that the person who is receiving your letter would respond best to correct, well-written English, and do your best to write for him or her! Write with feeling, though, or you will not be able to put over your experiences.

To sum up:

- Ask yourself what the purpose of your letter is.

- Choose a level of correctness and politeness suitable for someone who would care about these things.
- Be selective in your subject-matter.
- See also *Personal Experiences* in Chapter 3.

Laying out a Personal Letter

Marks may be available for the correctness of the way you set out your letter. It is also worth learning this skill because people may judge you on it in real life.

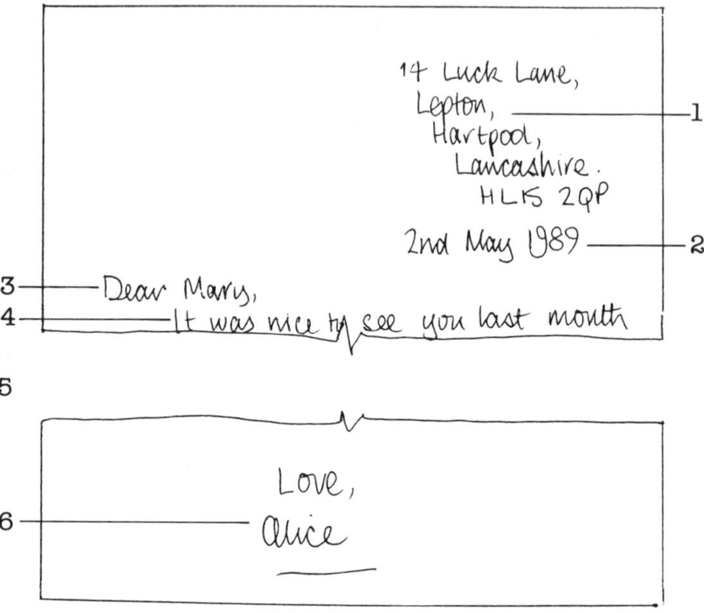

1. *Your address:* note the punctuation. *Do not* put your name at the top.
2. *The date.*
3. *"Dear . . .":* start this up against the margin.
4. *First paragraph:* Start this half an inch in from the margin (or more if your writing is large), and begin with a capital letter, despite the comma on the end of the line above.
5. *The second* and any *further paragraphs* should be indented in the same way as the first.
6. *Signing off:* don't use "Yours faithfully", "Yours sincerely" or "Yours truly". These are too cool and distant in tone, and belong in business letters. If you do not wish to end with "Love", use "Yours" or "with best wishes", or make up something for yourself.

Business Letters

In these, you are usually writing to someone you do not know, or do not know well, so you have to write as *correctly* as possible to create a good impression. Moreover, you have to hit exactly the right *tone* – calm, polite and impersonal – for dealing in a business-like way! Finally, business letters are often written to get something done (for example, to order goods): therefore, they have to be written *precisely* and *factually*.

Correctness

- Take great care over spelling, punctuation and any other mistakes to which you are prone.
- Study the following layout and use it *precisely* as a model, as office staff can be very critical about correctness.

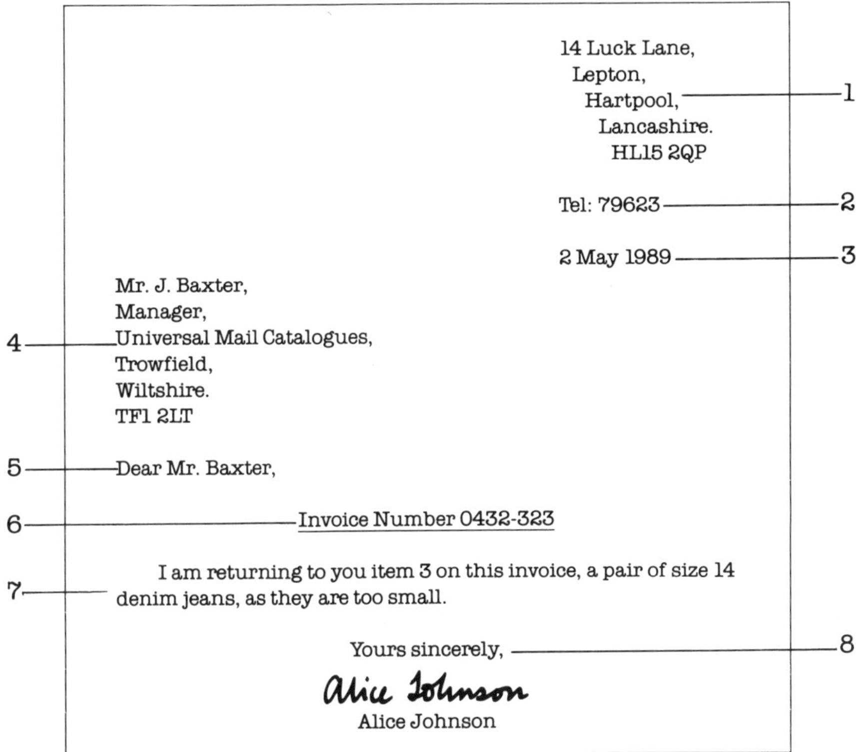

14 Luck Lane,
Lepton,
Hartpool, — 1
Lancashire.
HL15 2QP

Tel: 79623 — 2

2 May 1989 — 3

Mr. J. Baxter,
Manager,
4 — Universal Mail Catalogues,
Trowfield,
Wiltshire.
TF1 2LT

5 — Dear Mr. Baxter,

6 — Invoice Number 0432-323

7 — I am returning to you item 3 on this invoice, a pair of size 14 denim jeans, as they are too small.

Yours sincerely, — 8

Alice Johnson

Alice Johnson

1. *Address:* note the punctuation especially in the last two lines. Do not put your name on the first line; you may put the name of a firm here, though, if you are writing on behalf of them.
2. *Telephone number.*

3. *Date:* always write the month as a word.
4. *Receiver's name and address:* here, his position (Manager) has been included as a courtesy.
5. *"Dear . . .":* there are precise rules here.
   - Use *Dear + title and surname* (for example, *Dear Mr Baxter*, *Dear Ms Brown*) for a friendly effect. Always finish the letter with *Yours sincerely* (note the small *s*).
   - Use *Dear Sir* or *Dear Madam* (note the capitals) if you know you are writing to one person, but don't know his or her name. Use *Dear Sir/Madam* if you don't know the person's sex. Always finish these letters with *Yours faithfully* (note the small *f*).
   - Use *Dear Sirs* if you are writing to a firm or an organisation, but don't know who will receive your letter within that firm. Finish with *Yours faithfully*.
6. *Heading:* this is optional, but is an excellent way of making the subject of your letter clear.
7. *Opening:* indent this half an inch (or more, if necessary), and start with a capital. *The second* and any *further paragraphs* should be indented in the same way.
8. *Signing off:* see the rule in 6 on page 50. You should not really need to print your name under your signature in a neatly handwritten letter, but your signature should be readable. A typist would type your name under the space for your signature, however. A woman might follow her signature with *Ms*, *Mrs*, or *Miss*, but a man should not put *Mr*.

Businesslike Tone

Imagine receiving the following letter:

> *Dear Ms Smith,*
>
> *Once again I'm forced to write to your awful company. The car I bought from you has broken down seven times now, and I'm furious! How many times do I have to bring it back to you? Look: if you don't get it right this time, I'm going to send the boys round . . .*

The anger certainly shows through here, but are you sure you would not find the letter ridiculous? It is best if business is done in a cool, polite tone. Try to feel calm, detached and polite as you write!

- Here are some words and phrases which will help you achieve a business-like style:

  Thank you for your letter of . . .
  In reply to your letter of . . .
  Please supply me with . . .

I should be grateful if . . .
It would be convenient to . . .
I am pleased to . . .
I regret that . . .
Please accept my thanks/apologies/kindest regards.

Planning Business Letters

When you plan a business letter, you are aiming most of all to give factual clarity; your reader needs to understand exactly what it is you have to say. Most business letters aim to get the reader to do something: they may contain an order for goods, a request, or perhaps a complaint. This also needs to be planned for, so that it comes over clearly.

To allow the reader to see *precisely* what the letter is about, you can start with a *heading*. If it contains factual details, such as an invoice number, a customer number, or the *name* of a product, so much the better.

The first sentence or so of a business letter should act as an *introduction*: it should state clearly what the letter is about, and, if the letter is a reply, should refer plainly to the date of the letter which it is answering. Then you can briefly *develop* what you have to say.

Finally, to *conclude* your letter, politely yet precisely make the request, order or complaint that is the point of the correspondence. Check the letter over, and sign it.

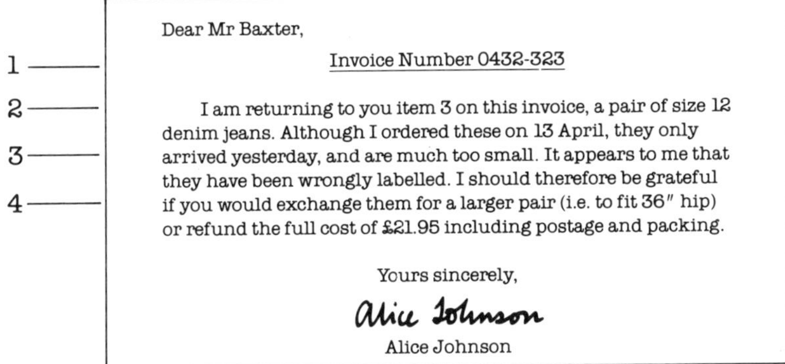

Dear Mr Baxter,

1 — Invoice Number 0432-323

2 — I am returning to you item 3 on this invoice, a pair of size 12 denim jeans. Although I ordered these on 13 April, they only
3 — arrived yesterday, and are much too small. It appears to me that they have been wrongly labelled. I should therefore be grateful
4 — if you would exchange them for a larger pair (i.e. to fit 36″ hip) or refund the full cost of £21.95 including postage and packing.

Yours sincerely,

Alice Johnson

Alice Johnson

1. *Heading:* see above. Note the factual precision gained by quoting the invoice number.
2. *Opening:* state the nature of the business. Use dates, names, facts and figures to make your statement precise.
3. *Explanation:* the details of the business in hand.
4. *Request:* write down *precisely* what you want done. Again, use facts and figures when possible.

Letters for Publication

The letters columns of newspapers and magazines offer an opportunity for ordinary people to air their views in public. Letters to editors are like short essays of argument, and should be planned as such.

- If you are asked to, lay out your work like a business letter. (You may not be asked to put in the address, etc., however.)
- Model your letter on a serious local or national paper, *not* a popular tabloid, where the letters may be much too short, and too sensational in tone.
- See *Putting Over Points of View* in Chapter 3.

Newspaper Reports

Grasping the Reader's Attention

A quick glance at the newspapers will show you that they are as different from one another as chalk and cheese! This chapter deals with writing reports for relatively serious papers: unless you are asked to do so, it would be unwise to write a report as if it were for a tabloid.

News reports have special characteristics, which make them fulfil their purpose, to interest their readers. It is no good writing an accurate report if it does not grasp the reader's attention and get him or her to read it.

Try to identify the following features in the example printed opposite.

1. *Headline:* short, neat, factual.
2. *Sub-heading* (optional): longer; explains the first headline.
3. *Opening paragraph* gives the basis of the whole story, so you will know whether you want to read it all.

£800 for HOSPICE FUNDS
High School Pupils' High-Speed Bed-Push

The St. Mary's Hospice Appeal was last night over £800 better off owing to the efforts of Hartpool High School pupil Jeanne Wharton (16) and her classmates.

Their charity bed-push round Hartpool town centre on Saturday netted a total of £832, a record for High School charity events.

Jeanne, of Radley Drive, Hartpool, organised the bed-push as a relay event. "I thought this would give it a speed and impact other events lack," said Jeanne, "but I never expected it to bring in so much money."

The push was started at 2 pm in Lion Square by Head Teacher Mrs. Anne Crawley.

Four teams took part, one from each of the school houses. Each relay team took a hospital bed once round Lion Square, along Kings Road to Albert Dock and back, before handing over to their classmates.

"I am very proud of my pupils' pluck and initiative," said Mrs. Crawley. "It shows what the young people of today can do."

4. *Hard facts:* names, places, dates, ages, figures, give the article the appearance of being true. Names of local people may make people relate to the story.
5. *Stress on the unusual* in the event you are reporting.
6. *Quotations* from people involved in the story bring it alive. Make the things they say brief and dramatic. (In real life, reporters often rewrite them.)
7. *Finishing on a strong idea* to reward your readers for reaching the end.

Some general points:

- Use short sentences and short paragraphs: newspapers try to be snappy and easy to read.
- Do not write a report which is too long-winded: papers try never to be boring.
- Do read and model your work on a serious national or local paper.

Instructions and Advice

IF EVERYTHING ELSE FAILS, READ THE INSTRUCTIONS.

Style and Approach

If you are asked to write a piece on how to do something, your first question ought to be, *Who am I instructing?* Children or adults? Beginners or experts? On your answer will depend:

the level of detail you use;
the difficulty of language you write with.

- Instructions need to be neither too difficult nor too easy for the reader.

If you have no other information, assume that your reader is adult, but a beginner.

Aims

Your first task is to decide exactly what you want your reader to be able to do. It is best if you can come up with something specific – *to bake a Victoria sponge* rather than *to bake a cake; to fix a wooden shelf to a wall* rather than *to put up shelves.*

- It is easier to write clear instructions for a closely defined aim.

Secondly, carry out a task analysis. In list form, write down in order everything that has to be done. (If you know about algorithms or flow diagrams, use these skills.)

To fix a wooden shelf to a wall

1. *Measure space.*
2. *Buy plank, wall plugs, screws, and brackets.*
3. *Get drill, screwdriver, pencil.*
4. *Measure height of shelf position in three places.*
5. *Join heights with line. . . . etc.*

Having sorted out the order of points, divide the instructions into stages: Steps 1 – 3 above might be thought of as *Stage 1: Preparations.* Once you have done this, you are ready to write out your instructions in full, using one paragraph for each section.

Full Instructions

First measure the space available for your shelf, and then buy a plank or piece of plastic-faced board of the right size. You will also need to buy a fixing bracket for every metre length of shelf, and sufficient wall plugs for wall brackets. You will need long screws to go into the wall plugs, and short screws to go into the shelf. The equipment you require will be a drill with a masonry bit suitable for the wall plugs, as well as a fine bit, a screwdriver, a carpenter's ruler, and a pencil.

Measure the desired height of the shelf, and mark it on the wall in three positions. Draw a line joining these three points. . .

Alternatively, write the instructions in check-list style, with numbered points.

Check-list

1. *Measure the space available for the shelf.*
2. *Buy a plank or piece of plastic-faced board of the right size.*
3. *Accessories: a bracket for every metre of shelf length; wall plugs; long screws for wall fixing; short screws for shelf fixing.*
4. *Equipment: a drill with a masonry bit suitable for the wall plugs, and a fine bit; a screwdriver; a carpenter's ruler;a pencil.*
5. *Measure the desired height of the shelf, and mark it at three points on the wall.*
6. *Draw a line joining the points. . .*

The Things You Use

Sometimes a task will involve collecting together a lot of equipment or things to use. In these cases, it helps to break up your plan, and perhaps your finished instructions, into two sections:

1. *The things you need;*
2. *The tasks you do.*

The time-honoured model for this is the recipe, with its two sections *Ingredients* and *Method*.

Date and Oat Flapjack
Ingredients
60 g (2 oz) butter or margarine
120 g (4 oz) porridge oats
60 g (2 oz) demerara sugar
60 g (2 oz) stoned dates
1 tablespoonful golden syrup
Method
Melt the fat in a saucepan, then stir in the sugar and syrup until it has all melted. Remove from heat and stir in the oats until the mixture is stiff, then stir in the dates. Press into a greased shallow tin so that the mixture is about 1 cm (½ inch) thick. Bake at 375°F (190°C, gas mark 5) for 15 minutes, then allow to cool. Cut into portions whilst still warm and soft. Remove from tin when fully cooled.

At other times, instructions may involve operating a complicated machine or device – such as when you tell someone how to operate a cassette recorder or camera. Once again, two sections are handy in this case:

1. *Description of the device*
2. *The tasks you perform.*

- Break down tasks into steps.
- Separate things you need from tasks to perform.

Practical Advice

You may need to write an essay or article which has practical advice as its basis, without being as precise as a set of instructions. This could include such topics as:

1. *Write an article giving advice and information on starting a hobby, sport or pastime of your choice.*
2. *Write an informative article on your school or college for new pupils or students.*

Aims and Readership. These need defining in the same way, and for the same reasons, as in detailed instructions.

Plan. When you know your aims, you can plan out what practical points you want to make. Each point should be supported by reasons or evidence, like those in an argument essay.

Gaining interest. If your advice is for beginners or outsiders, you need to capture their interest and persuade them of your point of view. One way of doing this is by adopting an enthusiastic tone. To do this well, you need to *feel* enthusiastic! Another technique is to back up your advice with personal experiences – little stories which bring home the meaning of what you are saying:

When taking a portrait of someone, part of the art is to work quickly and keep the conversation flowing, so that your subject does not become stiff and embarrassed. I remember having to pose for family photos when young, whilst relatives would fiddle for minutes with complicated cameras, and I would feel my smile stiffening into an unnatural grin. I still cannot bear to look at the photos they took. If, on the other hand, you can work quickly, you will get really informal and natural results.

It may occur to you that this book is basically a mixture of advice and instructions. That is why so many of the examples include personal experiences.

- Plan your advice.
- "Sell" your viewpoint.
- Bring in your personal experiences.

Directed Writing

Directed writing is the name given to the type of exercise where you are given a page or more of printed material, and are asked to make use of some of the material in it in a piece or pieces of writing of your own. The printed material might include:

passages of writing
pictures
diagrams
graphs
statistics

and you will have to select from these the facts or ideas that are relevant to the task you have been set.

Types of Exercise

The material you are given and the tasks you are set can vary widely. In effect, creative response questions to books, plays and comprehension passages are a form of directed writing. This chapter concentrates on factual and practical exercises.

Making Notes

At the basis of most of these exercises lies the skill of rewriting facts and arguments in your own words. The best way to approach this is by making a methodical set of notes from the material you have been given. Note-making is essential for similar reasons in many types of comprehension and creative response exercises (see Chapter 5), so it is a skill well worth developing. You may even come across directed writing questions which may need to be answered in note form. The scripts for certain types of oral communication exercise are written as notes (see Chapter 6). Finally, of course, good notes are essential for your revision for many of your GCSE exams!

What Notes Are For

Most often, you make notes to remind yourself of something you already know in outline because you have just read it, heard it, or thought it up for yourself. Notes of this sort can be very short, and often need to be taken in at a glance. They should therefore be carefully laid out on the page so that you never lose your place in them. Notes may need to be complete or selective: that is, they may need to represent all the main ideas in the text or lesson from which you are working, or they may need to pick out only one aspect of it which is relevant to the question you are going to answer.

Notes are especially important when you are asked to put part of a document into your own words, or to transform it from one use to another. They allow you to separate the gathering and selection of ideas from the rewriting, so that when you come to produce your version of the text you can concentrate on matters of style and correctness. If you try to work directly from a text you will probably produce a jumbled and ugly result, but if you take the time to make some notes first, you will have a chance of writing something that sounds fluent and natural. It is essential to work solely from your notes, and to look back at the original only in emergencies, or its style will infect yours.

Notes in Action

Suppose you were given the following text from a leaflet on an outdoor pursuits centre, and the question which follows it.

AIREDALE LODGE

Near Skipton, North Yorkshire

Airedale Lodge is the ideal centre for outdoor pursuits courses and weekends for schools, colleges and youth organisations of all types. Situated at Beck Hall, the Victorian mansion of the Hardacre family, it has a pleasant location in open countryside in Upper Airedale, yet is close to the Craven Fault and other notable geological features. Only five miles from Malham Cove and Tarn, it provides an excellent base for walking, climbing, or scientific pursuits. For biology students, the nature reserve at Malham Tarn will be of special interest.

The hostel-style accommodation is furnished in a bright, modern manner. Up to forty young people sleep in the small rooms, each of which accommodate between four and six in bunk beds.

Smaller rooms are available for group leaders. A well-equipped kitchen is available for guests' use; those under 18 must be supervised whilst cooking. A coin-operated laundry is available to deal with muddy clothes. There is a comfortable common-room for relaxation, with armchairs, a drinks machine, and colour television. The adjoining games-room has table-tennis and pool tables.

The centre offers a fully-equipped scientific laboratory and a modern class-room, each seating thirty, and the Warden can loan to schools an extensive range of climbing, caving and orienteering equipment, including waterproof clothing and a limited supply of walking boots. An assault course has been laid out in the grounds.

For further information, including charges, write to or telephone the Warden, John Hawksworth, at Airedale Lodge Centre, Scotton, near Skipton, North Yorkshire. (Tel. Airedale 24242).

Write a letter to the parents of a class, persuading them to send their children for a five-day biology field-trip to Airedale Lodge, from the 5th to the 9th April. The cost, including food, will be £35. Pupils must bring a sleeping-bag and pillow-case, and strong footwear.

You can see that this task involves selection: only those facts relevant to students and parents need be mentioned, and only those relevant to a biology course. How, then, can you note these down in a neat, easily readable form?

The key techniques are to:

- Use a title;
- Use a numbered heading for each topic; and
- Lay your work out on a page with only one fact on each line.

Let's see how this works out in practice: here is a set of selective notes which will help toward answering the above question.

AIREDALE LODGE

1. Location

5 miles Malham Tarn Nature Reserve

2. Facilities

Sleeping for 40 in small rooms (bunks)
Kitchen for pupils' own use (supervised)
Coin-op. laundry
Common-room and games-room
Class-room and lab
Outdoor equipment on loan:
    waterproofs
    boots (limited supply)

Points to Notice

1. *Title, heading and numbering.* These make it easy to see the subject of the notes, and what the main topics are.
2. *Layout.* The use of underlining, blank lines and indenting to the right is important. It gives the notes a shape that you will remember, making it easy to find your way through them. The further to the right a line begins, the smaller is the detail it contains.
3. *Own words.* The notes have been made as far as possible without copying out chunks of the original text. This has the advantage of making you think more about what you are doing, and learning the subject matter better.
4. *Selection.* Details relevant to geology, geography or physical fitness courses have been left out, as have matters such as the address, which are only of use to the organisers at this stage.

To write the letter to parents, however, you will also need some facts from the *question*. You should jot them down with your other notes, and give them their own heading.

3. Practical Details

5-9 April
£35 inc food
Take:
  sleeping-bag
  pillow-case
  strong footwear

Finally, you need to decide on the order in which you are going to put things, the style or tone suitable for the task, and anything you need to consider about the format. Then you can start to rewrite your notes in the form of a letter.

- When making notes, consider how you are going to use them before you start
- When rewriting, study the question as well as the notes you have made.

Directed Arguments

This type of exercise will look something like this:

> A journalist interviewed several people on the topic of teenage drinking and made notes of the following views. Read them carefully and then write your own article on *Drink and the Teenager.* You may use the quotations or not as you wish, and you may add your own ideas.
>
> Tracey, 17: *"You don't necessarily go out wanting to get drunk or to break the law, but in most of the places you go to you're expected to buy a drink of some sort. Many people would buy a*

soft drink, say, in a pub, but they'd feel childish in front of their mates. The important thing about alcohol is that it makes you feel grown-up.''

Police Constable: *''The law is this: if you're under 16 you aren't allowed in a bar, although you may go into a room in a pub with adults if it isn't mainly a bar. From the age of 14 an adult can buy you an alcoholic drink to go with a meal, but not to drink on its own. You have to be 18 to drink if you're not eating a meal, or to buy a drink yourself.''*

Parent: *''I'm frightened about what young people might get up to when they've been drinking. I don't think they realise just how much it lowers your inhibitions. It's not just sex I'm thinking of: they could get into all sorts of trouble with the law – 'borrowing' cars comes to mind. And even if they're old enough to drive legally, they could drive dangerously.''*

The first thing to do is to read through the question and the arguments several times, carefully, until you are sure that you understand them. Then consider just what the question is asking you to do. Ask yourself especially if a particular form of writing is being asked for, and if you are being cast in a specific *role* or *situation*.

Roles and Situations

Frequently in Directed Writing passages, you are asked to imagine that you are a person other than yourself, or that you have a job or task which you do not have in real life. In this question you are to write as if you were a professional journalist, and it would help if you could compare the task you have been given to a real magazine article. you could also consider the aims of such an article, which might include grasping and keeping the reader's attention! An article which is simply written, yet strongly controversial, would fit the bill.

Planning

You will also need to use the planning skills you learnt when putting over points of view (pages 43-44). Here, when jotting down your ideas, you will need to take some from the materials you have been given, as well as adding some of your own.

Once your plan is complete, there is one last decision to make: are you going to quote the views you have been supplied with word for word, or are you going to refer to them without quoting them? The choice is yours, unless the question tells you otherwise. The danger of quoting the views, however, is that your essay may degenerate into a mere commentary on other people's ideas, and have no life of its own. In the case of this question, however, the fact that you are writing an article for a newspaper or magazine suggests that you should use quotations. They can be incorporated into your article like this:

> *One of the main problems facing younger teenagers is where to go for a night out. Most places other than cinemas seem to cater for slightly older people and to sell drinks. Tracey, who is 17, told us, "You don't necessarily go out drinking or to break the law. Many people would buy a soft drink in a pub, but they'd feel childish in front of their mates." It is this combination of pressure from sales outlets and pressure to appear adult which starts many young people drinking.*

Notice how the quotation has been shortened without distorting it.

- Read the question and materials and then read them again.
- Consider whether you are being set a given role or situation.
- Plan carefully.
- Research and discuss if possible.
- Fit your tone and approach to the question.
- Do not just give your comments on the views supplied to you.

Using Documents

This type of exercise gives you lots of factual information to deal with, and usually puts you into a given role or situation in which you have to adapt and reuse the information. Let us take an imaginary example.

COMMUNITY RADIO CASE-STUDY

Britannia Radio, one of the new generation of low-power local radio stations, is being set up in your area.

1. You are a reporter on the local evening newspaper, which is in favour of the radio station, and you have been sent Documents A, B, C and D, attached. *Write an article* of about 400 words showing Britannia Radio's good features for the local community.
2. You work in the advertising sales department of Britannia Radio, and you have read Documents A, B, C and D. *Write a letter* to be circulated to local businesses, inviting them to advertise on your station. Start with "Dear Trader" and end with "Yours faithfully" and your own name.

Documents Attached

A. Programme Schedule for the station's first week of operation.
B. Policy Statement for staff on types of programme to be broadcast.
C. Advance details of programmes for ethnic minorities.
D. Table of costs for advertising at different times and on different days.

(You would, of course, be given Documents A, B, C and D in reality.)

Situation

Both questions ask you to imagine a situation: the launch of a new radio station.

- What you write must be relevant in content and tone to the situation.

Role

Both questions ask you to imagine that you hold a position relevant to the situation: in one you are a journalist, and in the other you are an advertising sales executive.

- Everything you write must be suitable in content and tone for the role you have been given.

The newspaper feature must really read like a newspaper article: it must have headlines and quotations, and should preferably be linked to an event so that it is a report of news. Its tone must be neat and clear.

The letter must have the formality of a business letter, yet still read encouragingly. It must use the facts given about the station's ethnic coverage, as well as giving some idea of the cost of advertising.

Readership

One way of making a directed writing task realistic is to consider what type of reader you are being asked to write for. In this example, the newspaper article asks you to write for ordinary people, but the letter asks you to write for a readership of local tradespeople. In each case, write only about what will be of interest to that particular reader.

- In brief, writing based on roles must be as realistic as possible.

Notes and Plans

All Directed Writing must also reflect the source-documents accurately, and many tasks like the one above require a great deal of detailed rewriting. You should therefore base your plan on a selective but accurate set of notes, and in examination conditions time should be left for this. *Never* rewrite long sections of an exercise direct from the source-material, as this makes it hard to achieve a good style.

- Notes and plans are essential for accurate work.

5 Reading and Responding

Why Comprehensions Are Set

"A comprehension – Oh no!" This is a common response when a teacher sets a comprehension exercise, and in some ways it is understandable. In fact, comprehensions are designed to test and help teach the following vital skills in understanding what you read:

1. *Vocabulary.* Questions may check on your understanding of individual words and phrases.
2. *Fact retrieval.* Short, simple questions will test whether you can recognise and reproduce simple factual statements.
3. *Hint-taking.* Other short questions will see if you can spot things which are merely hinted at in the passage.
4. *Summarising and paraphrasing.* Longer questions will ask you to select aspects of the passage in question, and reproduce slices of information in your own words.
5. *Analysis.* Sometimes, in the longer questions, you will need to re-interpret the material as you write it – for instance, by reorganising it into categories.

6. *Reasoning.* Questions which ask you to provide your own reasons for your reaction to a text check up both on your understanding of the piece and on your ability to think logically about it.
7. *Empathy.* Questions which ask you to continue a story, or retell it from a different viewpoint, invite you to take the point of view of one of the characters. Questions which ask you to write on a similar topic to that chosen by the author invite you to respond to the style, techniques or content in a way which is your own.

Let us have a look at how these work out in a sample comprehension.

Read the following passage and answer the questions on it, using your own words as far as possible.

Dictionaries may not be used.

York – Capital of the North

If you are about to visit York, you had better cast aside all your preconceptions about northern England. You will find no grimy black buildings here, nor mills, nor wild moorland. York sits comfortably in the middle of a rich and pleasant plain, and is built of timber and russet brick. If you look at it from a distance you will see a haze of pink-tiled roofs surmounted by the silver-white towers of its Minster, or cathedral. York is a unique city, and its history is still visible as you visit it.

As you approach from the south, you will drive along a broad tree-lined road, and then, as you near the centre of the city, you will find yourself alongside a vast open area, the Knavesmire. This is now York's racecourse, but is still technically Micklegate Stray, one of the city's medieval commons. If you drive on approaching the city centre, you will first of all pass large Victorian villas and then opulent Georgian town houses, for York was once the North's centre for polite society and social life.

Soon your progress will be brought to a full stop by the towering Micklegate Bar, one of the City's four medieval gateways. Stretching away on either side are the city walls, built in gleaming white stone, which form a scenic walkway round the town centre. Inside them is a tightly-knit and intricate pattern of medieval streets, narrow and crooked, using every inch of ground. Much of the property inside the walls is still medieval in origin, though it may not all look so at first. In almost every street you will see timbered houses with overhanging upper storeys, many of the best examples being in Stonegate and The Shambles, where the buildings almost seem to touch above your head. Many of the other houses and shops you will see are also medieval, although they don't look it, for in the Georgian and

Victorian periods it became the fashion to put up brick facades on the fronts of old timbered buildings. Keep a look-out and you will see the tell-tale signs such as timbers showing in end walls.

The city's real significance in medieval times was as much ecclesiastical as commercial, as the city's twenty or so surviving churches will show. The See of York took in a vast area – the whole of northern England – and its holder was in a position of real power. The Minster, therefore, has always been one of England's most important churches, and it grew throughout the Middle Ages to become the biggest and perhaps the most beautiful. Constructed of limestone, its exterior blends styles from Early English to the Decorated of the fifteenth century into a harmonious whole, dominated by a central tower which is both massive and delicate. Clustered in the square mile around it are other churches, all with some architectural distinction, such as the glorious glasswork of All Saints, North Street, or the higgledy-piggledy box pews of St. Mary's, hidden behind a row of houses off Goodramgate.

By medieval times, the city was already old. The Romans had settled here, at the most easterly practical river crossing of the River Ouse, and had built a fort from which to rule northern Britain. Emperors Constantius Chlorus and Hadrian stayed here, and legions were billeted here to police the territory and subdue Scottish raiders. The legend is still told of the Ninth Legion, who set off to quell a border invasion, never to be seen again – except, perhaps, as ghosts.

In the Dark Ages, the Vikings arrived, and in the last twenty years the remains of their town with its wooden houses, workshops and wharves has been excavated. You can see it reconstructed in great detail (down to the sounds and smells) in the famous Jorvik exhibition – Jorvik being the Vikings' name for York. After the Vikings came the Normans, who built York Castle, and once again used the town as a centre for controlling the North, at first through a fire-and-sword policy which left much of the countryside virtually uninhabited. One of their two keeps still stands guard over the eastern end of the town.

It was at the very end of the Middle Ages that York became once more England's northern capital. Henry VIII chose to govern this part of his kingdom through the Council of the North, and this was housed at the King's Manor, a rambling brick building situated off Exhibition Square. Now used by the University of York, parts of it are open to the public on application at the porter's lodge. In the seventeenth century, the Manor had its moments of glory again, when Charles I briefly held court there.

In the eighteenth and early nineteenth centuries, the town went through a quiet phase, until the coming of the railways, when George Hudson, the so-called 'Railway King', chose it as a major centre. York Station, built in 1877, is an architectural marvel, with its light, elegant train-shed built on a curve in the track. You can still get off an express train here, having travelled direct from London or Edinburgh.

Now York is to an extent living in the past. Since the 1960s the tourist industry has become more and more important, and the town has become more and more crowded in summer. It's not really surprising: the past is around you everywhere in buildings, museums and antique shops; nor is it such a bad thing, since the city is kept neat, tidy, freshly painted and prosperous by the tourists' money. There are still quiet corners, too, where you may find yourself alone in the ruins of a Norman house, or gazing at a medieval guild's ceremonial hall. In my mind, York is northern England's capital still.

Types of Question

1a. Give the meanings of the following words as used in the passage:

preconceptions (paragraph 1)
facades (paragraph 3)

b. Give the meanings of the following phrases as used in the passage:

tightly-knit . . . pattern of . . . streets (paragraph 3)
on application at (paragraph 7).

2a. What was the Knavesmire in the past, and what is it used as now?

b. What was the main purpose of the Roman settlement at York?

3. Using paragraph 1, give reasons for supposing that the author does or does not like the city of York.

4. What do we learn of York in the eighteenth and nineteenth centuries (the Georgian and Victorian periods)? Answer in no more than 80 words.

5. Describe the major phases of York's history. Answer in approximately 100 words.

6. To what extent would you like to spend a holiday in York? Give three reasons for your answer.

7. Write about a place you have enjoyed visiting. Your answer should cover about one page of A4 paper if you have normal-sized handwriting.

Steps to Follow

One of the main ways to success with comprehension exercises is to make a thorough, methodical job of answering the questions. You need to be aware of exactly what you are being asked to do, as well as of what the passage says. Go through the following steps as you work.

1. *Read the instructions at the head of the passage* and ask yourself:
   - Must I use my own words in all cases?
   - May I use a dictionary?
   - Is there a strict time-limit?
2. *Read through the passage at least twice*. On the first reading, concentrate on getting the general sense of the passage, and on the second, try to work out the meaning of any words or phrases that you find difficult. This will be useful even if you are not specifically asked about one of them in a question, because it will help you to understand the passage better as a whole.
3. *Read through all the questions before starting.* This will often enable you to see fine differences between the questions, and allow you to avoid repeating ideas in two answers when they should appear in only one.
4. *Attempt each question.* You need not answer them in the order in which they are set. So if you find a question to be very difficult, do not waste time on it – leave it until last. In this way, you can be sure of picking up marks on the questions which you know you can do.
5. *For each question:*
   - *Identify what type of question it is.*
   - *Read the question carefully.* Many people lose marks by answering questions which are not on the page!
   - *Estimate the length of answer required*, using any length-restriction stated or the number of marks available.
   - *Decide whether to use notes before starting your answer.*
   - *Use an appropriate technique, selected or adapted from the following pages.*
   - *Number your answer* but do not copy out the question.
6. *Check your answers for:*
   - *Factual accuracy*.
   - *Relevance to the question:* does what you have written really answer the question?
   - *Good English:* some marks will be available for the quality of your self-expression.
   - *Accurate copying of names and phrases from the questions.*
   - *The consistent use of inverted commas round any quotations.*

Model Answers and Comments

The instructions at the head of the comprehension passage require you to use your own words. This is important, and you should take it to be the case in all comprehensions unless you are told otherwise. Only through using your own words can you show that you have understood a passage. In this comprehension about York, you are not allowed to use a dictionary.

Question 1 – Defining Words and Phrases

Q.1a. Give the meanings of the following words as used in the passage:
preconceptions (paragraph 1)
facades (paragraph 3)

If you do not know the answer to a question of this sort, intelligent guesswork can help a great deal (see the section on meanings, page 9).

INTELLIGENT GUESSWORK

A.1a. Preconceptions *means ideas which you hold about a subject before you get to know about it at first hand.*

If you did not know the meaning of *preconceptions*, you might well have been able to guess at it in two ways: (1) The prefix *pre* always means before, and *conception* will remind you of *concept*, a thought; (2) in the next sentence, we are given examples of beliefs which have to be cast aside, and they are all beliefs about the North which are widespread.

Facades *means decorative fronts of buildings.*

Once again, intelligent guessing will help with this answer. *Facade* might remind you of *face*; whilst the context makes it obvious that the word refers to the front of a building.

If in these cases you had been allowed to use a dictionary, you might have obtained several possible answers from it – for example:

> Facade . . . *n* 1. the face or front of a building 2. *fig.* outward appearance, especially a false or misleading front concealing reality or intended to deceive.

In this case, the type of intelligent guessing suggested would help you to choose the right alternative.

- Use the context to guess the meaning of the word shown, or to relate it to the passage.
- It sometimes helps to compare the word to others it resembles, and to see if you can relate them to the passage.
- Be selective with dictionary definitions.

Q.1b. Give the meanings of the following phrases as used in the passage:

tightly-knit . . . pattern of . . . streets (paragraph 3)
on application at (paragraph 7).

A.1b. Tightly-knit . . . pattern of . . . streets *means the close, intricate way in which the streets fit next to one another,*

or

Tightly-knit . . . pattern of . . . streets *means that the streets fit together in an intricate layout.*

This type of question involves giving the meaning of a phrase rather than a single word. Note the use of dots to show that words have been missed out: you do not have to define them. The process of arriving at an answer is similar, however. Notice that I have not tried to translate *streets:* it is a simple, everyday word and to change it would obscure, not clarify, the meaning. The basic difference between the two answers is the word *that*, in the second one. Answers which include this word tend to be easier to write, but less exact. Using a complete sentence for your answer, beginning with the phrase you are defining, helps to ensure that your answer is a clear one.

On application at *means if you ask at.*

The context makes it clear that you have to do something at the porter's lodge, and common sense would lead you to suppose that what you have to do is ask. This answer is better than the following one:

On application *means if you apply to*

because *application* and *apply* are really forms of the same word. An answer like this would really be like answering the question *"What is a cat?"* by saying, "That's easy, a cat is a cat!" At least you would be a stage further if you had said "A cat is a small, furry mammal that makes the sound *miaow*."

- Do not repeat forms of important words from the question-phrase in your answer.

Question 2 – Discovering Facts

Q.2a. What was the Knavesmire in the past, and what is it used as now?

A.2a. The Knavesmire is today used for horse-racing, and in the Middle Ages it was used as common land.

Q.2b. What was the main purpose of the Roman settlement at York?

A.2b. The main purpose of the Roman settlement was to provide a base from which to govern northern Britain.

These questions simply ask you to dig out some simple facts, already stated in the passage. Such questions should always be answered in your own words as far as possible, to show that you have understood what you have read – so that 'as a racecourse' has become 'for horse-racing' in answer (a). Other transformations: 'medieval' has become 'in the Middle Ages'; 'rule' has become 'govern'.

Notice again that the answers are complete sentences, and begin with a phrase from the question. This is an excellent way of enabling you to check that your answer really is relevant to the question as set.

Question 3 – Taking Hints

Q.3. Using paragraph 1, give reasons for supposing that the author does or does not like the city of York.

A.3. Reasons for supposing that the author likes the city of York are that he describes its location favourably as "comfortably in the middle of a rich and pleasant plain", and that he gives a pretty picture of its colours: "a haze of pink-tiled roofs surmounted by the silver-white towers". Finally, he describes York as unique, and implies that you should visit it for its historical sites.

In this question you are being asked to pick up hints from the passage – to look at the feelings behind what is said. In questions like these, we often need to quote words from the passage *in order to comment on how we react to them*. Such comments are the statement that the first quotation seems favourable, and that the second is pretty. Note that the words quoted are put inside inverted commas. The last hint is explained without quotation.

Question 4 – Summary

Q.4. What do we learn of York in the eighteenth and nineteenth centuries (the Georgian and Victorian periods)? Answer in no more than 80 words.

In questions like this, you are asked to select several facts or ideas from the passage, and form them into a short paragraph. You should note whether a word limit has been set: if so, you will be marked down for exceeding the limit. Actually, a stated number of words is useful to you, rather than the opposite, as it will tell you whether you are including too few, too many, or roughly enough ideas in your answer. Only note down facts and ideas which are relevant to the meaning of the question.

- Use word limits to gauge whether you have the right number of ideas.
- Remember to be selective: read the question carefully.

A.4. The eighteenth and early nineteenth centuries were a quiet period for York, although it was a social centre for the rich, and many large houses were built. It was also the fashion to modernise timbered buildings by putting a brick front on them. Then came the railways, brought by George Hudson, the 'Railway King', who chose York as a centre. The station was built in 1877, and is excellent architecturally, with a well-designed train-shed built on a curve. (80 words)

This answer was built from the following notes. See how I have changed the order of ideas in the final answer, so as to get them into a clear order based on time. Notice also the two-stage change from the original's wording to my own. Not only are summaries clearer when they are in your own words; they also show the examiner that you understand what you are writing.

York 18th-19th Centuries:
Large Victorian villas, rich Georgian town houses
North's social centre for polite society
Fashion to put new fronts on old timbered buildings
A quiet period until mid-19th C.
Railways: George Hudson, the 'R. King' chose it as centre
Station built 1877
Architecturally brilliant, well-designed train-shed built on curve.

Question 5 – Summary with Analysis

Q.5. Describe the major phases of York's history. Answer in approximately 100 words.

Basically, the technique for this question is like the last one, with one addition: you are asked to concentrate on classifying the information into historical phases. This sort of analytic question often comes up in passages about people, when you need to classify information under aspects of their characters. Here, it is quite easy to spot the historical periods and put them in order: the problem is to know how much to say about each one. The question helps us, however: notice the tight word limit.

A.5. The Romans built a fort at York from which to rule the north of Britain. Then in the Dark Ages the Vikings built a town here. The Normans built castles, and in the Middle Ages the town's gateways and Minster were constructed as the town became a centre for church and trade. At the end of the Middle Ages the Council of the North sat here, and in the seventeenth century Charles I's court briefly met here. The eighteenth and early nineteenth centuries were quiet, but in the Victorian age the city became a railway centre. Since the 1960s it has increasingly become a tourist attraction. (106 words)

Question 6 – Reasoning about the Passage

Q.6. To what extent would you like to spend a holiday in York? Give three reasons for your answer.

This question tests your ability to think about the passage logically, applying your mind to it in detail. You need to know what the passage says about York and give your opinions about it. So the first step is to ask yourself what sort of a town it is. Your list of ideas might include the following:

Pretty
Historical
Full of old buildings
Minster
Jorvik
Railway station

Once you have a list, select those ideas which mean something to you, and write your opinion of them, stating your reasons as you go.

A.6. York seems to be a very historic place with many ancient buildings, including the Minster. Even people who are not keen on sightseeing could not fail to find something of interest in the city.

Since York is a railway centre, it might be a good place from which to take day trips, which would suit people who like to spend time in the country or at the seaside.

Question 7 – Creative Response

Q.7. Write about a place you have enjoyed visiting. Your answer should cover about one page of A4 paper if you have normal-sized handwriting.

In some questions of this kind, the examiners are simply hoping that the passage will have set your mind working and that you will be able to write a page or so of good, lively, essay work: this is certainly the case here.

In other cases, though, you are asked to take the ideas of the text more thoroughly into account. The tell-tale signs are phrases such as

taking the author's views into account

or

comparing your ideas to those in the passage.

To do questions of this last type well, you will need to have a list of basic ideas in front of you as you write, as in Question 6.

A third type of creative response requires you to step inside a character's mind and write from their point of view. An analysis of his or her character is necessary here. The examiner is interested in how imaginatively you can build on it. More help can be found on the techniques for this sort of question in the section on longer creative response exercises at the end of this chapter.

Reviewing Novels

'The Great Gatsby' by F. Scott Fitzgerald is the story of Nick Carraway and his neighbour Jay Gatsby, who lived on Long Island, New York, in the 1920s. Nick goes one day to see his cousin Daisy Buchanan and her husband Tom, and there he meets Jordan Baker, a tennis star, with whom he begins to fall in love. Soon, he gets to know his neighbour, too, when invited to one of Gatsby's huge, expensive parties. Later, when he meets Jordan in New York, she tells him that Gatsby is in love with Daisy . . .

Too many review essays are like this: the writer feels an irresistible urge to tell the story, and gets bogged down in minute, and often irrelevant, detail. Ask yourself: if you were wanting to find out whether you would like a particular book or film, would you want to be told the whole story? Probably not: it would ruin any suspense the plot might have. So begin your review with only a brief statement of what the plot is about: the following would be long enough.

'The Great Gatsby' is a story of love and rejection set on Long Island, New York, in the 1920s. It tells of Jay Gatsby's attempt to recapture Daisy, a rich girl who had jilted him five years earlier to marry Tom Buchanan, a playboy polo player.

So what else can you write about? The real subject of a review is the quality of the text or the performance, so you need to work out *why you enjoyed it* (or why you didn't!).

- Never simply retell the story in a review.
- The basis of a good review lies in the comments you make.

The plot. The first thing to ask about a plot is whether it holds your attention. Plots may be realistic, or they may relate more to your fantasies; in either case, they need to have interesting, perhaps surprising, things happening in them. You can make points about plots quickly and neatly, like this:

The plot of 'The Great Gatsby' gets under way slowly, as Fitzgerald is paying more attention to establishing the book's mood and characters in our minds. Once it gets started, however, it carries us quickly forward from the sordid and realistic scene in which Tom Buchanan confronts Gatsby with his gangster past, to the tragic end in which both Gatsby and Tom's mistress, Myrtle, lie dead.

- Comment *briefly* on the nature of the plot: mention just a few details.

The mood. Many stories have a characteristic feeling about them – tragic, comic, romantic, or tense, for instance. Longer stories may have a range of such intense emotions. A story which involves our feelings strongly in this way will also keep our attention. You may wish to make several comments like the one which follows, to show the range of moods the author is capable of conveying. Notice how a quotation is used in the paragraph below: the technique of using a brief quotation plus a comment to explain it is basic to writing reviews of books. When you are reviewing a performance of a play, or a film or television programme, you can use descriptions of what you have seen instead.

The novel takes in romance and tragedy, but perhaps its characteristic mood is the frenzied excitement of Gatsby's society parties: 'The large room was full of people. One of the girls in yellow was playing the piano, and beside her stood a tall, red-haired young lady from a famous chorus, engaged in song. She had drunk a quantity of champagne . . . She was not only singing, she was weeping too.' It is a glamorous world, but one in which no one is sure of his or her true emotions.

- A story's emotional power is often its most compelling aspect.

The main characters. The attraction or repulsion which we feel for these is part of the fascination of reading or viewing, and we need to be able to write about its basis. As with plots, we can relate to characters either because they are realistic or because they appeal to our fantasies. The important thing in either case is that there should be something intriguing or unusual about them. The points you make should be backed up by short references to the story, and, if you are writing about a text, the major ones should be reinforced by brief quotations. (If your quotations are too long, your reader cannot tell precisely which bit you are commenting on!)

Jay Gatsby is the central character of the story, and despite any early doubts the reader might have, is definitely its hero. Coming from a poor background near Chicago, he possesses a determination to be successful which shines through the resolutions he wrote down as a young person: 'No more smoking or chewing. Bath every other day. Read one improving book or magazine each week.' When hard work did not pay off, he turned to the underworld to make the money needed for him to be Daisy's social equal. This gives him a mysterious appeal. "They say he once shot a man,'' one of his guests tells us; and though this may not be true, the nature of his friend Meyer Wolfshiem makes us suspicious.

Your analysis of a hero or heroine could be much longer than this: indeed, it could be the main feature of your review. To analyse characters clearly, it helps to have a good vocabulary: consider if you could use the following words effectively and correctly. If not, look them up!

altruism	egoism	introversion	selfishness
calmness	emotionality	love	sentimentality
courage	escapism	pride	shallowness
cowardice	extraversion	realism	vanity
cruelty	heroism	romanticism	volatility
cynicism	intensity	sadism	wisdom

- A story's characters can be one of its easiest and most satisfying aspects to write about: often it will form a major part of your review.

Meaning. At the deepest level, a book, film or play often is satisfying because it means something to you; and some comment on a book's significance, as you see it, makes a good opening or conclusion to your review. To do this, you need to think about the basic nature of the main characters' experiences in it. If you are lucky, the author may have spelled this out for you towards the end of the story in one of the following ways.

1. The hero or heroine may come to some realisation about what has been happening (see Fiction in Chapter 3).
2. A minor character – someone who observes the main story – may be made to comment on the hero or heroine's life.
3. The author as storyteller may comment.

Many stories do not have these devices, and occasionally you will come across one in which the comments are *ironic* – that is to say, you are intended to disbelieve them. In these cases, you will have to make up your own mind. In *The Great Gatsby*, however, it is Nick Carraway who learns the lesson. You might write:

> *What is it, then, that gives the death of this gangster heroic status? It is his ability to hold on to his illusions, as Nick Carraway points out when he says, ''Gatsby believed in the green light, the future that year by year recedes before us. It eluded us then but that's no matter. . .'' The world pushes Gatsby in the opposite direction to his romantic dreams, and the final impact of the book is of great pathos at the impossibility of Gatsby's acting out his romantic impulses.*

If a story has no such statement, you need to look for patterns in the plot which reveal what the author was thinking about. If two or more characters have very similar experiences, or if two characters seem to have strongly contrasted experiences, you can be sure that the author intended you to think carefully about this. In the novel *Wuthering Heights*, both the hero, Heathcliff, and the heroine, Catherine, die as a result of the extreme intensity of their emotions: both are reduced to states in which they in effect take their own lives. The members of the next generation in the family, however, have much gentler characters, and at the end of the story we feel that they have a good chance of living happily. From this we can conclude that the authoress, Emily Brontë, meant the story to tell us about the destructiveness of passion and the life-giving properties of a gentler attitude to life.

- Stories are generally written with some sort of meaning in mind: it can help a reader if a reviewer gives his or her impression of what this meaning is.

Reviewing Performances

When you are reviewing a performance of a play, or a film or television drama, in addition to the things already mentioned you need to write about the quality of the production.

Acting. In all three types of review, the acting is an important element. Have the actors been well chosen for their parts? Do they look right in age, physique, and facial appearance? Are their voices right for the parts they are playing? Do they move correctly? Is their acting convincing, or are they over-acting, overdoing gestures and changes of voice? A paragraph on an actor might read like this:

> *Rodney James, acting Hamlet, was a weak point in the production through being too old for the part. Hamlet behaves like a young man, but James was rather clumsy in the final duel scene. Too often he threw his speeches away by muttering them. With him in the main role, the whole production could hardly succeed.*

Production values. Other aspects worthy of comment include the

quality of the costumes and sets, and, in film and television, the photography. It is the job of the producer or director of a performance to make all these factors, together with the performances of the actors and musicians, add up well and serve as an interpretation of the writer's ideas and feelings. If you have read the text of a play which you have also seen, or if you have read a novel or story which has been adapted into a play, film or television feature, you can comment on whether you think the production reflects the story as the original author saw it.

Adaptations of plays into films often contain many extra scenes, since the cinema can show outdoor scenes just as well as indoor ones. In addition, stage plays are mainly about people talking, whilst we are used to films showing lots of action, so action scenes are often added and the characters' words are cut. You can consider whether the film has the same sort of impact as the original play – whether or not it is faster-moving, funnier or more thrilling, even whether its overall meaning has been changed.

The changes made when novels are adapted into films or plays are usually in the direction of shortening and simplifying the story, as novels tend to be more complicated. In addition, the director has to find actors and actresses who are more or less like the characters described by the novelist: in the original novel of *Far From the Madding Crowd*, for instance, the hero has light-coloured hair and the heroine dark, whilst in the film he has dark hair and she is a blonde! Nevertheless, in their character-acting the performances are excellent, and this would be worth commenting on.

- View each aspect of the performance as an interpretation of the work, and say to what extent you think it was successful.

Creative Responses

When you have read or watched something, you may be asked to write in one of the following ways:

1. Write a story of your own with similar characters, a similar setting, or a similar theme.
2. Write a sequel (what happens next to the characters).
3. Retell part of the story from the point of view of one of the characters.

Questions like these can come in coursework when you have been reading a play or story, or, in examinations, they can follow a comprehension passage. To do one of these tasks well, you need to review the story *in your head*, asking yourself the questions in the last sections. Only then will you be able to see the aspects of the story that you need to emphasise in your response.

The difference between this form of writing and a review is that it asks you to step inside the character or characters that you are writing about and see the world from their viewpoints, as well as from your own. It also sets you free to imagine more of their world than the author has actually set down, or to compare it with life in the present day. You need to approach the writing of this kind of essay as if you were writing your own fictional story, once you have thoroughly understood the original author's plot, characters and ideas. Marks will be awarded for the general quality of your writing, and whether your story is a good one in its own right. Other marks will depend on whether you have continued or developed the original passage's characterisation, meaning and mood. For instance, if you were asked to write a scene in Nick Carraway's later life, you would have to make his character, thoughts and attitudes grow out of the ones he has as a young man in the novel. It might begin like this:

> *Now I am approaching retirement I can look back on a satisfying and full life. When I last wrote about myself, when I was telling poor Gatsby's story, I was still shocked by the way his life had ended. It certainly showed that life held no short cuts to success or greatness, but it also showed that those people who had achieved these things were no more worthy of them than you or I. If it had not been for Daisy Buchanan's selfishness and Tom's cruelty, Gatsby might still be alive today. It was this sense of disillusionment which led me to abandon New York, and travel back West to my home town; and it has been a decision which I have never regretted.*

- Creative response questions are invitations to look at the characters in a story from within, to show that you understand them and their world.
- Check whether a question requires you to write entirely within the scope of the original story, or whether it allows you to add scenes, ideas or characters of your own.

6 Oral Communication

Oral Work

All the GCSE English syllabuses feature oral work: for the first time, it has been given priority in British education. As you may know, you will receive *separate* grades in written English and Oral Communication, so that, for instance, a poor grade in oral work cannot bring down a good grade in written English. On the other hand, you do have to achieve a grade in *both* parts: if one of them is ungraded, the other will not be graded either.

We spend our waking lives talking (and teachers spend a great deal of time in silencing their pupils!), so why is it necessary to teach and test oral work? It is true that we talk a great deal of the time, but most of this

talk is informal, between friends and relatives who know one another intimately. We can use informal language in these circumstances, and our friends can guess a great deal about what we mean to say. The difficulties come when we are talking in more formal contexts – in discussion groups or committees, or when we are giving a talk to an audience. In these circumstances, we have to be as clear as we possibly can, and make an effort to understand and be understood. It is for circumstances such as these that the Oral Communication syllabus is trying to prepare you.

Accent

Oral communication is not an attempt to teach 'BBC English' or elocution. It is recognised by the examiners that almost everyone speaks with some sort of regional accent, and that these cannot and should not be wiped out. So do not worry if you have a regional accent as long as you can be understood by someone listening to you.

Dialect, Slang, Colloquialisms

On the other hand, dialect, slang and colloquialisms do cause problems in Oral Communication, just as they do in written work (see Chapter 1). All your oral tasks will be set in a way that requires your language to be apt for a given situation – and this situation will normally be a formal one, even if you are taking part in it along with your friends. By calling a task *formal*, we are saying that it is a type of task which you might have to undertake with strangers in real life, so that in doing it you will need to make your meaning as clear and well-developed as possible, as well as keeping to a polite tone of voice.

What Your Assessor Is Looking For

To some extent, of course, this will vary from task to task; but there are some general, positive features which make for good communication between people.

Confidence

Needless to say, some people have more confidence than others. Some can stand up in front of an audience without the slightest tremor, whilst others get the quakes if anyone other than their friends is listening. Confidence *can* be acquired, however, by practice. This practice needs to feel reasonably safe for you, though, and you will do better practising with a teacher whom you trust, and a group of class-mates you get on with. If you cannot manage this, try practising oral tasks at home with your family and friends – anyone, in fact, who will help you if you get stuck and will give you a kind but frank opinion on how well you are doing. With solo tasks such as giving a talk, or reading aloud, you can gain confidence by making a cassette recording and listening to it. For

this to work properly, however, you need to imagine your audience as you speak, and use the same strength of voice as you would use to a real audience.

Apart from your confidence showing in the skill with which you listen and speak, it will also show in the way your general behaviour reflects your mood. Two important aspects of this are your body-language and your voice quality.

Body Language

It is very easy to tell a great deal about someone's inner feelings from their posture, their ways of moving, their gestures, and the way they look at people. Nervous people tend to fidget a lot, which detracts from what they are saying, and they often avoid looking at the person or people they are talking to, which makes them look shifty.

Voice quality

A good speaker's voice will sound just loud enough, and will be pleasant on the ear. Nerves, however, can make you want to whisper or shout, or make your throat feel tight so that you want to clear it often.

Exercises

Sometimes, if you have been told that some aspect of your verbal communication needs attention, this can make you even more nervous and self-conscious. Occasionally, students dry up completely – and if

you are to achieve a grade in Oral Communication, you have to say *something*! Practice with people who help you feel confident is therefore very important, as are games, exercises and activities which your teacher may introduce. At first sight, they may not seem to have a lot to do with Oral Communication, but they have the aim of helping you *feel* all right about performing, for as usual your inner feelings are the key to doing well. Here are a few exercises that you can try out with groups of friends, or alone, before tackling an oral session.

Relaxing Your Body

Sit comfortably in an armchair and direct your attention to the muscles all over your body. Are they tense? If so, then *you* are tense, and need a little relaxation. Close your eyes, then clench your toes, stretch them out, then let them relax. Next, bend your ankles in one direction, then the other, then relax. Thirdly, tense your calf muscles, then let them go. Carry on, working up your body, and finally finish by screwing up all your face muscles, then letting them go slack. Finish with a deep outward breath, and sit still for a moment. (You can do most of this exercise in secret, if you need to.)

Breathing

If nerves make your chest tight, or make you breathe fast, then use the following method of slowing down your breathing. This method can be done in any position, but is best done sitting comfortably, or even lying down. Breathe in slowly, using your diaphragm to pull in the air, rather than expanding your chest. Hold your breath for a second; then let it out gently. Repeat this thirty times.

Loosening Your Inhibitions

Games to do this need to be done with a group of others. These games can be purely physical, or they can involve performing; they are intended to help you feel that working with others is fun. Here are two examples:

1. *Stamping on ants.* The group of you stands in an open space. You imagine that the floor is covered by swarms of biting ants and that you must stamp on them all before they bite you. Keep this up until you begin to feel tired!

LOOSENING YOUR INHIBITIONS

2. *Charades.* Act out charades in which, in turn, each of the group mimes the syllables of a word or phrase – as in the show *Give us a Clue*. If you wish, score the game by playing in teams.

Producing Your Voice

Stand up and stretch your throat by bending your neck backwards as far as it will go (not too violently!); repeat this three times. Then bend your neck forwards until your chin is on your chest; repeat again; finally, tilt your head four times to the right, then to the left, as far as it will go. Go through the whole routine once again. Then say slowly, with the lowest notes your voice will make, "Oooh, aaah, oooh, aaah" several times.

- Don't reject games and exercises as silly: they *do* help you unwind.
- Nerves *can* be overcome – confidence *can* be gained.

Sensitivity To The Situation

Oral Communication tasks involve you in a situation which may be real or imaginary. The situation may be that you have to discuss something with a friend or a group of class-mates; or you may have to give a talk to a group. These are real situations, like the following:

> 1. *What are the root causes of football violence? Discuss this with your group. Do not try to agree on a single answer, but explore any ideas the group has. You will then be able to use some of these ideas in an essay.*
> 2. *Give a talk to your group on an unusual experience you have had – an adventure or an achievement, for example. Your aim is to grasp their interest.*

Much of the skill in dealing with situations such as these lies in feeling at ease and predicting how your audience will react – what they will be interested in, what they will accept, how hard you will have to work to make them understand your viewpoint. It is also vital to react to your audience's behaviour as you speak: this means keeping your eyes and ears open, and taking in their reactions to you. Finally, it involves listening to the others in discussions and question-and-answer sessions. All this underlines the fact that Oral Communication is almost always a two-way process.

Other situations are imaginary: you or your audience may have to play a role in them.

> 3. *You are the leader of a Scout/Guide troop: work out a programme of outdoor activities for a camping weekend.*
> 4. *There are four of you in a lifeboat twenty-one days away from land, but there are rations for only three people. Decide what to do.*

Here, you need to react to the imagined situations, and to the type of person you are playing. In this kind of situation, experience of acting and of games which lower your self-consciousness is definitely an advantage.

How will your sensitivity show to the assessor? He or she will be looking above all for appropriateness of behaviour: the right degree of correctness and formality, a use of vocabulary which is neither too childish nor too difficult for your audience, and a sense that you are taking in messages from the others and not just talking to no one in particular. You should seem at ease, and your voice should be expressive – neither dull and bored nor jerky and nervous.

- Sensitivity involves looking, listening and predicting.
- In imaginary situations, take your role seriously.

Oral Tasks

Tasks vary in formality and in type, but normally they are geared at some stage to two-way communication. Some sample tasks follow.

Pair Discussion

Here you are given, or asked to choose, a partner and asked to discuss a topic. This is the least formal type of task, and in it you are free to use colloquial vocabulary, and so on. There are two possible types of discussion: ones in which you merely explore a topic, and ones in which you have to make a decision. In both of them you should keep a check on the discussion's *relevance*: you will lose marks if you drift off the subject or spend all your time on one detail. If you have a decision to make, keep a check on time, and shortly before the end remind your partner that this has to be done. Be willing to compromise and listen: you may lose marks by simply pushing forward your own ideas.

You will be given marks for the following:

Ability to develop your ideas. The major things which you say should not just come out as brief chunks of information: you should be prepared to expand on them, even to go over them two or three times if your partner looks lost.

Turn-taking. You should neither dominate the conversation by talking too much, nor remain silent. If you are forever butting in, this is a danger-sign, unless your partner is trying to dominate you. Wait until your partner is ready to pause before making a statement of your own. If you have a silent partner, you will gain extra marks for trying to help him or her to come in on the discussion.

Paying attention. Discussions work only if you listen to, and talk about, your partner's views, and compare them with your own. Failure to do this is very serious, and underlines once more the point that communication is about listening as much as about speaking.

It is possible to do some preparation for a discussion session, although it is also possible to be over-prepared. If you come with a long list of things which you *must* say, you will not listen or turn-take properly. Nonetheless, it can help if you make a list of topics to cover, and your basic thoughts on them. You *must*, however, be prepared to change your plans – and even your mind – as a result of discussion.

Group Discussion

This exercise is one degree more formal: indeed, the larger the group, the more it has to use rules of behaviour and language. Ideally, for GSCE, you should be working in groups of four or five.

The marking of group discussions is very similar to that of pair discussions, but turn-taking and paying attention are even more important. In particular, if you help to keep the discussion on course, help quiet group-members to join in, and show that you are listening to everyone's viewpoints, you will gain extra credit.

In group discussion, some people have bad habits, such as objecting to everybody else's ideas, being sharp and sarcastic, or defending their own ideas, right or wrong. All these habits destroy good discussion and are likely to lead to a substantial loss of marks. If your discussions are taped, listen to them and see if any of these faults occur in them. Remember that the offender may be *you!*

In discussion:

- Think about the topic in advance.
- Don't dominate.
- Don't stay silent.
- Develop your thoughts.
- Keep a check on whether what is being said is relevant.
- Be as positive in attitude as possible.

Giving a Talk

Here, the situation is even more formal, and your language will reflect this. You will be expected to produce a slang-free, colloquialism-free performance, and to accompany this with confident, non-verbal communication. Fortunately, this is not as hard as it sounds!

The key to a good talk is *good preparation*. You *must* know your subject well, and you *must* have a clear idea of what you are going to say, and the order in which you are going to say it. If your talk is about a personal experience, you will be able to plan it out in your head; but if your talk is factual, or is intended to teach something, you may need to research the topic. In both cases, you should produce a rough plan, like that for an essay, as the next stage.

What you need is a script for your talk, a script that will allow you to be expressive as you speak, to look at your audience, and to break off and answer questions as they come up. The worst possible way to attempt this is to write out a speech word-for-word and read it out, because:

1. reading aloud is a difficult task in its own right;
2. it prevents you from looking at your audience;
3. it is easy to get lost if you are broken off;
4. it is inflexible, and prevents you from changing your plan in response to your audience.

Learning such a speech by heart is almost as bad; the *only* time these techniques are appropriate is when every word must be weighed extra carefully, as on occasions of great legal or political importance.

The ideal script from which to give a talk is, in fact, a set of well laid out notes. These can be brief, as they are there to remind you of things you already know; and if they are laid out neatly, you will be able to glance up and down from them without losing your place. You will be able to modify what you actually say in response to your audience's mood and interest, and according to the time available.

Here is a set of notes for a talk on choosing a camera. The notes are intended to be easy on the eye, using plenty of white space, capitals, and underlining, and contain both the main ideas and any hard facts it is necessary to know.

Talk – Choosing a Camera

Three types of camera
(Hold up specimen of each as it is mentioned.)
(Explain meanings of names.)
Cartridge-loading (110)
35 mm Compact
35 mm Reflex

1. *Cartridge-loading camera (110)*

ADVANTAGES	size
	weight
	easy loading
	ease of use
	price – cheapest of all
	prints and slides
	fair for action photos
DISADVANTAGES	'grainy' pictures, not very sharp*
	less intense colour
	being phased out.

2. *35 mm Compact camera*	
ADVANTAGES	medium size and weight ease of use automatic flash (Show flash.) all but the cheapest have – automatic exposure – automatic focusing therefore better quality, sharp, bright pictures good for enlargements* prints or slides
DISADVANTAGES	more expensive: £60 – £200 for good quality harder to load and unload the film
3. *35 mm Reflex camera*	
ADVANTAGES	most flexible type of camera range of lenses: wide-angle, telephoto, zoom* offers most control over results* through-the-lens viewfinder good for close-ups* bright, clear prints and slides*
DISADVANTAGES	size and weight price (£100 – £1000 +) hardest to load requires skill to use to full advantage

CONCLUSIONS
Assess your needs
budget
willingness to learn skills
(Pass round fact-sheet.)

* (Pass round appropriate prints and comment on them.)

Notice the use of *visual aids* – the cameras themselves, and the prints made with them. These help focus the audience's attention if you can use them neatly and confidently, and if you talk about them. Most talks can be improved by using pictures, demonstrations or diagrams. You may wish to use the blackboard, an overhead projector, or to play a cassette: each of these involves forward planning, and getting your teacher's help.

Finally, notice the use of a fact-sheet or hand-out *at the end*: these are valuable in any form of teaching; again, however, you will get credit using one only if you introduce it and comment on it.

- Use a script in note form.
- Plan your talk like an essay.
- Choose your subject to suit your audience.
- Stay in contact with the listeners.
- Use visual aids and hand-outs when they are relevant.

Question-and-Answer

Normally, your talk will be followed by a session in which you answer questions from your listeners, or discuss points made by them. In addition, you may find that they will interrupt your talk to get you to clarify something, so you need to be on your toes in order to answer them. Marks are awarded for many of the skills found in discussion situations: your answers should be well developed, and show signs that you are really paying attention to what has been asked. You should allow yourself time to gather your thoughts if you need to: you can say, ''Let me think about that for a moment,'' whilst you sort out what to say.

- Give thoughtful answers to questions and comments. Take your time.

Ready, Steady, Go

So, you are in your group, sitting or standing comfortably, and it's time for your talk to begin. You feel confident, and you have a script. How do you begin?

The skill here is to *take charge* of the group. Assume it will do what you want it to do. Smile, tell the group you are about to begin, and, in a voice loud enough to be heard, announce your topic, glance at your script. . . and you're off. If you get lost as you talk, pause briefly to look at your paper. Glance at your listeners, especially at their reactions to jokes, to important points you make, or to visual aids. Be prepared to change your plans as you go along.

Don't let the talk peter out: you should end on an interesting point, and in any case you can announce the ending with a sentence such as, ''That is all I have to say, so now we could go on to your questions.''

When the questions are dying down – or at the end of your allotted time – again, take charge: tell the group that the talk is over, and thank them for listening. Finally, you might try the hardest thing of all – asking them, ''How did I do?'' Gathering their reviews of your performance can be one of the best ways towards doing better next time.

- It is your talk: take charge – but . . .
- Keep aware of your audience
- Invite *friendly* comments and learn from them.

Reading Aloud

In many ways, reading out a passage is the hardest of the oral skills, since the ideas and feelings you are expressing are not your own. Three main areas of your performance will be assessed: clarity, fluency and expressiveness.

Clarity. Can your voice be heard by everyone in your group? Nerves may have caused you to drop your voice to a mere mumble, or to have covered your mouth with a hand. Other habits leading to a muffled sound are looking down as you read, or holding the book in front of your face. The most helpful ways round these problems are those which increase your confidence; otherwise, sit or stand up straight, wear your glasses if you are short-sighted, and make sure you are familiar with what you are going to read.

Fluency. Good readings should be without halts, hestitations, false starts and mispronunciations; and to get rid of these, adequate preparation of your text is necessary. First of all, read it through and make sure you understand every word of it: if you do not, then get help. Also check that you can pronounce all the words confidently; again, get help, or use a dictionary. Finally, read the passage aloud, preferably tape-recording it, and check that you are phrasing it intelligently (see the section on the sounds of full stops and commas in Chapter 2). If you are having trouble, mark some extra commas in positions where a slight pause may make sense; then, practise, practise, practise! If you have been able to make tape-recordings of yourself, listen to them at least once without the passage in front of you, and check the speed of your reading. Could someone who had not seen the passage take it all in from your reading, or are you gabbling? Fluency is not the same thing as speed of delivery!

Expressiveness. The big advantage which Oral Communication has over writing is that you can use your voice to underline the feeling or mood of a piece. Every passage has *some* feeling, even if it is only the business-like mood of a piece of scientific or legal information, or a set of instructions.

Mostly, however, you will be given passages which demand more expressiveness than this. Ask yourself what moods are present in your passage, and how to express them. Here is a small extract for you to consider:

> *"She's sure to survive!" said Jane encouragingly. "She even managed to wag her tail as I carried her in."*
>
> *"She's a young dog still," I joined in. "Plenty of life in her yet." I hesitated, though, when I saw the blood on Jane's sleeve where it had touched the dog as she picked her up from the road.*
>
> *The door from the kitchen clicked open, making us jump slightly. The vet walked in. He looked at each of us slowly, before he spoke. "I'm afraid there's very little hope," he said, quietly. "There are internal injuries as well, and she's lost a lot of blood."*

If you read out this passage, you would need to express Jane's tone of encouragement in the first paragraph, perhaps by a firm, brisk reading, and light tone of voice. Then, in the second, you would need to modify this to express the author's faltering agreement – probably by slowing up, and reading more quietly, from "I hesitated. . ." onwards. Possibly the pitch of your voice would drop, too. In the last paragraph, you could start reading more vigorously again, emphasising the sound of "clicked" which made the characters start. Then there would be a strong contrast with the slow, deep, firm voice of the vet as he broke the bad news.

Thinking about this reading reveals the main features of expressiveness: speed, volume, tone and pitch. Listen to another pupil whose reading seems dull and lifeless, and you will see that it sticks to single speed, and keeps to the same volume, tone and pitch: it is like

music which repeats the same note endlessly. Expressiveness is not something that is sissy or "arty": it is the one quality which keeps your listeners awake whilst you read. Do not go overboard with it, however: it is quite easy to reduce your listeners to hysterics!

- Prepare your reading in advance, in particular checking
  - meaning;
  - pronunciations;
  - pauses.
- Practise your performance.
- Read expressively, with variations of pace, volume, tone of voice and pitch.

Index